I0518361

ISBN: 979-8-9992145-0-8

Printed in the United States of America

First Edition

Cover design by Nick Gumpert
Book design by Nick Gumpert

I dedicate this book to my wife. For allowing me the opportunity to keep pursuing things that fill my buckets and stay curious.

To my kids. To leave them with thoughts, ideas and techniques they can implement when I'm not around.

To you. For taking the time to read this book and invest in the single biggest differentiator for anything you do, your mindset.

And I'd like thank myself—for following through with this commitment and becoming something I never planned to be until just two years ago, an author.

The 4U Page

PART 3: CHASING HAPPINESS

INTRO

This is book 1 of 4. I thought about packing more than 350 mental tips, ideas and techniques into one big book, but that's not how you scroll, learn or grow. So I broke it up—in short and simple chunks. One focus at a time.

What if the biggest barrier between you and the life you're craving is the story you keep telling yourself?

Starting isn't about empty motivation or quick-fix positivity—it's about challenging the limiting beliefs living rent-free in your mind.

Imagine breaking free from the anxiety of perfection, escaping the crushing pressure of curated online lives, and silencing the nagging impostor syndrome whispering you're never enough.

You'll find yourself reflected in authentic, messy, and real experiences—struggling with perfectionism, endlessly scrolling, and never feeling "good enough." The turning points you'll witness aren't neat or polished; they're honest and raw, mirroring your own challenges with balancing dreams, family pressures, and the overwhelming quest for happiness.

This book is the next step in a conversation that started on my podcast *Mental*—but some stories need more than a mic. They need a moment. A page. A pause.

Each episode of *Mental* sparks a thought. Starting lets you sit with it, wrestle with it, and actually apply it. If the podcast is the spark, this book is the slow burn.

Starting isn't just stories—it's a blueprint. Your mental health isn't about merely surviving anymore; it's about stepping into the extraordinary life you genuinely deserve.

They say the best books aren't the ones you say were *so* good! The best ones are the ones that make you take action. I sincerely hope this influences you to do just that – in some way personal to you. Generally speaking, now is as good a time as any to say you're starting. Let's start!

If I believe I can,
I'm right.
If I believe I can't,
I'm right.

PROLOGUE

The kids sat at the kitchen table, arguing over something small — again.

Dad walked over, quietly placed three pots of water on the stove, and started boiling them.

His son raised an eyebrow.

His daughter asked, "Uh… are we making dinner?"

Dad chuckled, "Not yet. I want to show you something."

In one pot, he dropped **carrots**.
In the second, he gently placed **eggs**.
In the third, he poured in a handful of **coffee beans**.

The kids waited.

Five minutes passed. Then ten.

Finally, Dad turned off the heat and called them over.

He scooped out the carrots, then the eggs, and poured the coffee into two mugs.

"Alright," he said, "what do you see?"

"Carrots, eggs, and coffee," his son replied, obviously.

"Yup," Dad nodded. "But here's what matters — they all went through the same thing: hot boiling water. But each one reacted differently."

He handed his daughter a carrot.

"Feel this. Soft now, right? It started out strong, but the heat made it weak."

He gave the egg to his son and had him crack it.

"See? It was fragile inside, but now it's hardened."

Then Dad smiled and held up the coffee mug.

"But the coffee bean? It didn't just get changed by the water — it *changed the water*."

The kitchen went quiet.

"So," Dad said, "when things heat up — when life gets frustrating or feels unfair — you've got a choice. You can let it make you soft, make you hard... or you can be like the coffee bean and bring something good into the mess."

His daughter looked at the coffee and whispered,

"I wanna be the coffee bean."

His son nodded. "Yeah... but I think it takes practice."

Dad smiled. "Exactly. And know you don't have to get it perfect. You just need to keep showing up, every day — and over time, if you're mindful and intentional, you'll start changing your environment instead of being a victim of it."

PART 1

I WRITE MY STORY

I WRITE MY STORY

Your generation is drowning in advice about what to do, but no one's teaching you how to think. These stories aren't feel-good fluff—they're your modern-day cheat code to life to better navigate a world designed to break your focus, steal your time, and convince you that mediocre is enough.

You're not failing because you lack talent. Let's be honest, while you're making excuses, someone with half your ability is building the mindset that will leave you in the dust. The difference? They've learned to weaponize and embrace discomfort while you're choosing to avoid it at all costs because... it doesn't feel good. Spoiler alert – it never will. But when you decide to work through it, your future self will thank you for it.

Every app, every notification, every "quick scroll" is literally rewiring your brain for distraction and instant gratification. The students crushing it aren't smarter—they've just learned to protect their attention like their life depends on it. Because it does.

Forget your GPA. Your daily habits are writing your real resume. The way you handle stress at 16 becomes your leadership style at 26. The excuses you make today become the limitations you live with tomorrow. Your future boss isn't hiring your potential—they're hiring your habits.

While everyone else crumbles under pressure, the ones who make it treat pressure like rocket fuel. They've learned the secret: pressure doesn't break you—it reveals who you really are underneath all the comfortable lies you tell yourself.

The biggest risk you can take, is playing so safe that you never discover what you're actually capable of. The people changing the world aren't the ones who avoided mistakes; they're the ones who made more mistakes and learned from them faster.

You think you have forever to figure it out. You don't. Every day you spend consuming instead of creating, following instead of leading, is a day someone else is building the life you think you deserve.

The uncomfortable truth: Your generation has every advantage except the one that matters most—the mental skills to use them. Stop waiting for permission. Start investing in the biggest differentiator you'll ever have, your mindset. Starting will help you do just that.

To conclude each story, a SIQ Tip (simple, immediate, quick) is shared to challenge you to help you live an even better life, sooner.

MINDSET RESOLUTIONS

It's New Year's Day in Albany, NY, just another cold winter day for sixteen-year-old Jamie. She sits by her bedroom window, watching the snow gently fall, transforming the landscape into a serene white blanket. The house is quiet, her family still resting from the previous night's celebrations. In front of her, an open math workbook stares back at her, pages filled with complex formulas and equations—daunting symbols that seem to taunt her.

Jamie makes a resolution that morning: to conquer her math anxiety and stop feeling overwhelmed by numbers that mock her. She remembers being told when she was younger that the brain is like clay, capable of being shaped through effort. That idea once filled her with hope, but as the math grows more challenging, it starts to feel like a cruel joke.

The clock ticks quietly in the background as her frustration rises. Notifications ping from a group chat on her phone— friends are sharing jokes, enjoying another lazy winter break day. She's tempted to join them, to close her workbook and forget about the numbers. But today feels different. There's a resolve within her—a quiet determination to face the challenge head-on.

Jamie doesn't aim for perfection—just to understand. For twenty minutes, she works through one problem at a time, breaking them down into smaller, more manageable chunks. Time passes without her noticing. Slowly, in the middle of calculations, something shifts. It's not a grand revelation, but a quiet click—concepts begin to connect.

With half the day gone, Jamie has worked through a stack of problems. She feels in control—something she hasn't felt in a long time. Two weeks later, when her math test comes back with a bold "A" at the top, her heart swells. It's not just about the grade. It's proof: her mindset shift, her effort, her small decision to show up—it worked.

As she slides the test into her backpack, a new thought rises: What other limits has she accepted without questioning? How many barriers could she break... if she simply challenged them?

SIQ Tip: My brain is a muscle. The more I work it and the more I challenge it, the more solutions I will come up with and the more I will grow.

MICRO MOVES
It's a freezing Saturday evening in Mobile, Alabama, and seventeen-year-old Gio sits at his kitchen table, staring blankly at a stack of glossy college brochures. The weight of an entire future presses on his shoulders.

One choice, they say. One decision will set the course for his life. But that pressure—it's paralyzing. What if he chooses wrong? What if his entire future slips through his fingers before it even starts?

Scrolling mindlessly through forums on his phone, desperate for answers, Gio stumbles across something unexpected: "micro-decisions." And a single line catches his eye—*small, consistent actions lead to big change over time.* It's like a switch flips in his mind. What if this isn't about making the decision, but about making a series of small, meaningful ones?

The next day, with doubt, fear, and that lost feeling still looming, Gio tries a different approach. He makes a plan:

research one college each day, jot down his thoughts, and talk to someone who goes there. It feels simple, small—but doable.

As the days pass, each micro-decision chips away at the giant wall of anxiety. Slowly, clarity replaces fear. Each tiny step gives Gio more control, more confidence. He's not just picking a school anymore—he's building a future, one piece at a time.

But as Gio finally settles into his decision, a deeper realization hits him—what if the most important choice isn't *where* he's going, but whether he's ready to face who he needs to become to get there?

SIQ Tip: I'm just one choice from a new beginning and one commitment away from a new life.

FLEXIBLE IDENTITIES

On a warm spring day in Arlington, Virginia, 22-year-old Ana feels like she's slipping through the cracks of reality. Everything's off—her friendships, her sense of belonging.

She's tried it all: the wild, reckless party crowd where nobody even remembers her name the next day, and the academic grind squad obsessed with GPAs and zero personality. No matter where she goes, she's a chameleon—blending into spaces that never feel like home. Each day, the isolation deepens, gnawing at her like a ticking time bomb.

Then one night, after another mind-numbing hangout, she stumbles down a random street and spots a flickering sign that seems almost alive:
ART WORKSHOP – NO RULES, JUST VIBES.

It's like the universe whispers to her in that moment, daring her to dive into something real. She doesn't overthink it—she signs up.

The next day, she walks in expecting the usual—judgmental eyes and fake smiles. But what she finds is chaos in the best possible way. Paint splattered everywhere. Music blaring. People talking about everything from aliens to existentialism. These aren't average people. They're raw, unfiltered, and absolutely unhinged in the most brilliant way. For the first time ever, Ana doesn't feel like she has to wear a mask.

Weeks pass, and she's hooked. This isn't just an art group—it's a revolution. A tribe that sees through her layers and celebrates the madness within. She flourishes here, alive in ways she didn't even know she had shut down.

SIQ tip: My uniqueness is better than better.

A NOVEL IDEA
Liam watches his sanctuary die a slow, brutal death.

The Detroit Public Library branch he's loved since childhood is becoming a ghost town. Dust coats everything like abandoned dreams. The computers are so ancient they might as well be museum pieces. The only visitors are a handful of elderly regulars who whisper.

This place used to pulse with life. Now it's just... waiting to be forgotten. But Liam refuses to let that happen.

One afternoon, instead of mourning what's been lost, he starts scheming about what could be. What if this dead space becomes the heartbeat of the community? Gaming tournaments where kids actually want to hang out. Coding bootcamps that teach real skills. Movie nights that pack the place.

The head librarian, Ms. Reynolds, thinks he's delusional when he pitches the idea. A 14-year-old revolutionizing a dying institution? But something about his desperation convinces her to take the gamble.

Liam becomes a one-person army. He floods social media with pleas for donations. Corners local business owners until they cave. Rallies classmates who've never cared about libraries to suddenly care about this one. The response shocks everyone—tablets pour in, furniture appears, new books stack up faster than they can be shelved.

The turnaround is unexpected. Within a month, the library transforms from funeral home to block party. Kids who used to avoid the place like it's cursed now camp out for hours. Gaming sessions draw crowds. Coding workshops fill up instantly.

But here's the real magic: Liam doesn't just save a building— he creates something that never existed before. A space where learning feels like living, where community happens naturally, where being curious isn't weird.

The dying library doesn't just survive. It becomes the place everyone wishes they'd had growing up. And it all starts with one kid who refuses to accept that good things have to die just because they're old.

SIQ Tip: The world is changed by my example, not my opinion.

DATED DISCOVERIES

Five years ago, Josh discovers graphic design—and it feels like finding his soulmate. He becomes obsessed, spending every free moment mastering Photoshop and Canva, devouring design theory videos on YouTube, creating vibrant visuals that start racking up likes and shares. The validation is intoxicating. For the first time in his life, Josh feels genuinely good at something.

But then... he gets comfortable.

While the design world evolves, Josh stays frozen in 2020. He keeps using the same techniques, same templates, same fonts that worked before. Why fix what isn't broken, right?

At this year's design conference, everything shifts. A presenter showcases mind-blowing VR capabilities in graphic design—immersive experiences that make traditional concepts look prehistoric. The room buzzes with excitement. Designers are practically vibrating with energy. Everyone except Josh.

He sits there, completely lost—like he's watching a movie in a foreign language. While others scramble to take notes and exchange contacts, Josh realizes something brutal: he's the only one in the room who's not excited. The only one who feels left behind.

Walking back to his hotel room, Josh feels the weight of his own stagnation. He's been so proud of his early skills that he stopped growing. While everyone else levels up, he's been hitting replay on a highlight reel from five years ago.

The next morning, he does something that terrifies him: he enrolls in a VR design course. Downloads software that completely intimidates him. Starts following creators whose work makes him feel like a total beginner again.

It's humbling. It's uncomfortable. And it's absolutely necessary. For the first time in years, Josh feels that original spark again—the thrill of discovering something new, the fire that comes with pushing creative boundaries.

SIQ Tip: If I'm still excited about what I learned five years ago, I'm not learning anything new.

COINED GROWTH

In Portland, Maine, sixteen-year-old Emma wakes to the sight of a small wooden box on her desk. Inside are her "habit coins," each one representing a daily goal—practicing guitar, reading, running. Every coin she drops in feels like a step toward becoming someone better.

One evening, as she drops a coin for finishing her reading, her older brother Jake walks by. "You really think those coins are going to change anything?" he smirks. "It's not like you're going to become some kind of genius, Emma."
She pauses, her hand hovering over the box. "It's not about being a genius," she murmurs. But after he leaves, the thought gnaws at her. What is it about?

Weeks pass, and as her seventeenth birthday draws near, the coins pile higher. She sees changes—her guitar playing smooths out, her thoughts feel sharper. But something feels off. The coins stop being symbols of progress and start feeling like rules. Her life grows rigid, every action dictated by whether she can drop a coin at the end of the day.

One afternoon, while strumming a new song, she freezes. Looking at the box, a thought hits her out of nowhere: Is she actually becoming better—or just a slave to the routine?

That night, instead of dropping in a coin, she lets it fall to the floor. Then, she opens the box and spills the rest out, scattering them across her desk. She smiles.

Emma realizes it was never about counting achievements. It's about becoming—about who she's growing into, coins or not. They served their purpose. But now, she doesn't need them to see how far she's come.

SIQ Tip: Habits aren't about what I achieve, but who I become.

HABIT HARVEST
At 21, Mia sits on her porch in Boston on a calm fall evening. She takes a deep inhale from her vape, watching the cloud of smoke disappear into the cool air. She thinks back to when she was 16—vaping was just something fun to do with friends. Peach-flavored. Harmless. Everyone was doing it. She never saw it as dangerous.

Her mom once asked, "How much of our future is shaped by our habits rather than just the decisions we make?" But back then, that question didn't land. Vaping felt like a trend, not a life-altering choice.

Over the years, casual puffs become routine. She vapes while studying, on the way to work, and late at night before bed. It blends into her day—so automatic, she stops noticing. The vapor clouds feel comforting. And quitting? She tells herself she can do that whenever she wants.

Then the irritation in her gums starts. At first, she brushes it off—maybe she's brushing too hard. But the discomfort grows. A dentist visit leads to a referral. The specialist confirms what she's been fearing: gum cancer.

Sitting in the sterile doctor's office, the weight of her choices hits hard. That "harmless" habit? It's not harmless anymore. It's carved itself into her future—one she never saw coming.

That evening, staring at the vape in her hand, she faces a truth that feels undeniable: Her habits have been writing her future in invisible ink.

For years, she believed she'd shape her life with big decisions, career plans, and goals. But here she is—realizing a habit she picked up just to fit in has been steering the wheel all along. The future she thought she controlled has been quietly slipping away... one inhale at a time.

SIQ Tip: I do not decide my future; I decide my habits, and my habits decide my future.

GAME PLAN
At 17, basketball consumes Elijah's every thought. Making the starting lineup isn't just a goal—it's the expectation. He trains relentlessly on the nearby courts of New York City, but as tryouts get closer, his confidence starts to shake. His shots feel rushed, his movements lose their sharpness, and no matter how hard he works, the outcome he craves feels further and further away.

I WRITE MY STORY

One evening, after an intense individual session, Elijah sits on the edge of his driveway, sweat dripping down his face, the weight of doubt pressing hard on his shoulders. His dad walks up and sits beside him. After a long silence, he turns and asks, "Are you focusing on the little details, or just the end result?"

The question makes him reflect and ponder for a bit. Elijah realizes he's been so locked in on making the team, he's ignored the foundation—the small things that actually build his game.

The next day, he resets. No more frantic workouts or obsessing over the final outcome. Instead, he breaks his game down: footwork, dribbling, positioning on rebounds. Every piece matters. He builds a routine that targets the fundamentals. One detail at a time, he refines his rhythm. He works with his coach, asks for feedback, and trains not for perfection—but for progress.

When tryouts arrive, Elijah feels something different: calm. He moves with confidence and control, dialed in on each play, each moment. When his name is called for the starting lineup in the first game of the season, it isn't relief that sets in—it's pride. He's earned this opportunity, one small decision at a time.

Walking off the court after his first game, Elijah gets it. His dad wasn't just talking about basketball. The little things don't just lead to big moments—they *are* the big moments. And in mastering the details, he's created his own success.

SIQ Tip: My success isn't determined by the height of my goals, but by the systems I put in place and consistently do to reach goals I set.

LEARNING LADDER

Nicole and Madi start at the same competitive tech firm on the exact same day. Same entry-level position, similar backgrounds, nearly identical starting salaries. They even have desks next to each other after onboarding, so it feels natural to grab coffee and vent about the same impossible deadlines.

But after work, their paths split.

While Madi collapses onto her couch every evening, binge-watching Netflix and scrolling endlessly through social, Nicole chooses differently. She spends her evenings learning something—anything—for 30 minutes. Night classes on emerging tech. Online workshops on project management. Books on industry trends. Nothing massive, just steady curiosity.

At first, there's no real difference. They perform at similar levels, get similar feedback from their manager. Madi even jokes about Nicole being a "study nerd" when she skips happy hour for a coding bootcamp.

But as more time passes, the gap starts to grow and soon, starts to show.

Nicole begins pitching more innovative ideas in meetings. She speaks confidently about new tools and trends while others hesitate. When big projects come up, the managers turn to her—not because she's louder, but because she's ready.

Less than two years in, Nicole gets promoted to senior developer. Then she's leading a team, managing major clients. Meanwhile, Madi stays in the same role, watching from the sidelines.

And one day, it clicks for Madi. While she was coasting, Nicole was building. All those small daily learning sessions didn't just stack up—they exploded into career momentum. It's not that Nicole is naturally smarter or more talented. She just made different choices with her time.

Now, sitting at her desk in the same position two years later, Madi sees it clearly: Nicole's quiet commitment to learning didn't just change her title—it changed her confidence, her skills, and her entire professional direction.

SIQ Tip: Learning is the biggest degree of separation, and it's the only sustainable advantage I can create and maintain, if I choose.

RICH ROUTINES

On a gloomy summer morning in the outskirts of Denver, 23-year-old Jace sits across from his mentor—a man who effortlessly navigates the highs and lows of entrepreneurship. Jace feels like time is slipping away—he's already 23 and desperate to leave his mark. After months of wondering, he finally asks, "What's your secret to success?"

His mentor leans back, eyes sharp but calm. After a pause, he replies, "Jace, what are you willing to do in the moments that don't count for credit?"

The question stops Jace cold. He didn't expect a question, let alone that one. It lingers in his mind, gnawing at him like an unsolved puzzle. He shrugs it off at first, assuming there's some secret—some hidden strategy or bold move his mentor's holding back.

But as he watches more closely, Jace notices something unsettling: there are no flashes of genius. No grand breakthroughs. Just the quiet, almost invisible grind.

Every morning, his mentor wakes before dawn, reading industry reports. He asks relentless questions in every meeting, even the small ones. He plans each day with precision, never leaving anything to chance.
Success, Jace realizes, isn't glamorous. It's maddeningly simple.

Frustrated but curious, Jace begins adopting the same habits. Early mornings. Deep focus. Learning when he's tired. Planning when he'd rather rest. It's brutal at times—mentally exhausting and soul-crushing.

But then something starts to change.

Slowly, his confidence builds. Leadership opportunities start to appear. Others begin to recognize him. The struggle that once consumed him begins to fade.

That's when it clicks:
His mentor's question wasn't just about success. It was about grit. About what you choose to do when no one's watching. About the small, unglamorous actions that quietly shape who you're becoming.

SIQ Tip: Most 'secrets' to success are actually not secrets at all. They are just routines that go unnoticed.

REROUTED DREAMS

At 15, Ava's entire world revolves around becoming an architect. Growing up in a suburb of Austin, TX, she pours her heart into applying for a prestigious summer program at a top design school, believing it's her first real step toward the future she dreams of.

When the rejection letter arrives, it hits like a punch to the gut. Weeks of effort reduced to two words: Not accepted. Her confidence crumbles. For the first time, she questions whether she's cut out for the path she's always imagined.

For days, she avoids her sketchbook—too ashamed to even look at it. Her dream, once so vivid, now feels distant and unreachable. Then she spots a flyer at school: "Volunteers Needed: Help Design and Build a Community Garden." It's not glamorous. Not what she envisioned. But with nothing left to lose, she signs up.

When Ava shows up at the site, something unexpected happens. As she digs into the ground and works side by side with locals, her creativity begins to flicker back to life. But this time, it's not about portfolios or perfection—it's about people.

She sketches garden paths, designs seating areas, even proposes a space for kids to play. Each choice she makes isn't for credit or applause—it's for the community. And when she sees their excitement, something shifts. She feels purpose. Real purpose.

By summer's end, Ava's perspective is completely different. That rejection—the one that shattered her—now feels small. Architecture no longer means accolades and prestige. It means creating spaces that matter.

I WRITE MY STORY

Her failure wasn't the end of her story. It was a redirection—toward something greater, something real.

And for the first time in months, Ava feels alive again.

SIQ Tip: Sometimes not getting what I want is a gift.

MONEY MATTERS

Jenna grows up in a house where the clink of coins on the kitchen counter signals survival. In a rural Nevada town, every grocery trip is a calculation, every utility bill a reminder of how little they have. Her parents' constant struggle etches itself into her bones, igniting a fierce vow: *I will never live like this.*

By her early thirties, Jenna achieves what once felt impossible. Her tech startup flourishes—and so does her bank account. She becomes the success story she always dreamed of—a millionaire, far removed from the grinding poverty of her childhood. But success, she quickly learns, carries its own weight.

The higher she climbs, the more isolated she feels. Friends turn into distant acquaintances, their laughter fading into hollow echoes when she realizes they're more interested in what she can offer than who she is. Business meetings replace family dinners. High-rise offices feel more like home than her actual home. The money builds a fortress around her—but also locks her inside.

Her brother, Aaron, chooses a different path. He stays rooted in the same neighborhood, facing the same small struggles Jenna fought so hard to escape. One winter evening, overwhelmed by loneliness, Jenna drives to Aaron's house.

She sits in her car, wanting to go say hi as she watches through the window. Inside, Aaron and his family laugh around the kitchen table—the same table they grew up around. The warmth in that room, the effortless love, stings.

Her hand hovers over the car door, trembling. But she can't open it. In that moment, she realizes the truth: she chased wealth to outrun pain, only to collide with a different kind of emptiness.

As she drives away, tears blur her vision. She has everything she thought she wanted—but not the one thing money can't buy: a place where she truly belongs.

SIQ Tip: Being broke is hard. Being rich is hard. Choose your hard.

COMFORT COSTS

At 23, Hannah builds the perfect life in Phoenix—safe, predictable, comfortable. While her coworkers at the marketing firm dive into challenging projects and pick up new skills, Hannah sticks to what she knows. Same tasks, same routines, same cozy little bubble.

Her friend Sierra is the complete opposite. Sierra volunteers for every impossible project, learns software that fries her brain, and actually asks for criticism that stings. Hannah thinks she's crazy for making life so unnecessarily hard.

Then their company announces a massive expansion—and a promotion both of them want. Hannah feels confident. She has seniority, solid reviews, and three years of reliable work.

Sierra gets the promotion.

I WRITE MY STORY

Seeing the announcement email hit her inbox feels like a gut punch. Hannah has more experience—but Sierra has more growth. While Hannah's been playing it safe, Sierra's been building herself into someone they can't afford to lose.

The truth hits hard: Hannah's comfort-seeking has become career quicksand. She's been so afraid of failure, she's guaranteed her own stagnation.

That weekend, staring at Sierra's new office through the glass wall, Hannah makes a terrifying decision: she's done playing small.

She starts saying yes to projects that scare her. She wrestles with analytics software that makes her want to scream. She asks for feedback that bruises her ego but sharpens her edge. Every day feels uncomfortable—but that discomfort becomes proof she's finally growing.

Six months later, when another promotion opens up, Hannah's name is at the top of the list. Not because she played it safe—but because she got bold about being uncomfortable.

Standing in her new office, Hannah gets it now: she spent years clinging to the safety of staying the same—when all along, the real magic was in choosing to become something more. Growth hurts. But staying stuck? That hurts worse.

SIQ Tip: Do I want to be comfortable OR do I want to grow? Because I can't do both.

LOST MOMENTS

In the quiet town of Missoula, MT, 20-year-old Bella spends her nights chasing the life she once imagined—hanging out with friends, late-night parties, fleeting moments of freedom.

At home, her mother cradles three-year-old Noah, tucking him in every night, telling him stories Bella never heard herself. While Bella's out, clinging to the carefree youth she refuses to let go, her son grows up without her.

Each morning, Bella comes home tired—eyes heavy, heart indifferent. She glances at Noah, asleep in his small bed, but her mind drifts elsewhere. The life she dreamed of never included quiet nights at home, rocking a child to sleep. Her mother's gentle voice meets her in the hallway:
"He asked for his momma again tonight, Bella."
But the words barely land.

One evening, as Bella's getting ready to leave again, her mother stops her at the door. "Do you even know your son?" she asks, her voice trembling. "He's growing up, Bella. You're missing everything."

Bella laughs it off, brushing past her—too stubborn to let the truth settle in. But when she returns later that night, the house feels different—quieter, colder. She walks into Noah's room, expecting to see him fast asleep. The bed is empty.

Panic grips her chest. Then she sees the note, in her mother's handwriting, sitting on the sheets: "He needed someone who was here. We've gone to stay with your sister. Call in the morning."

Bella drops to the floor, the weight of her choices crashing all at once. Noah is gone.

I WRITE MY STORY

And for the first time, she feels the full depth of what her life has become—how empty it truly is without him.

SIQ Tip: The past is a thief: it steals the present and the future from me.

TIME OUT
Cam's life is written in headlines before he turns 18.

Five-star recruit. Full ride to the University of Miami. NFL destiny practically guaranteed. In Miami, he isn't just a high school football player—he's the golden boy carrying an entire city's dreams on his shoulders.

The future feels bulletproof. College stardom, draft day glory, generational wealth—all mapped out like a GPS route to greatness.

Then his body betrays him.

The exhaustion starts small. Just feeling drained after practice. Then comes the pain that won't quit, the bruises that won't heal. What should be a routine physical becomes the day his world implodes: stage four leukemia.

In one doctor's visit, everything evaporates. The scholarships, the stadium lights, the NFL dream—all reduced to a medical chart and a timeline nobody wants to discuss.

For weeks, Cam disappears into grief so deep it feels like drowning. This isn't supposed to be his story. This is supposed to happen to other people, not the kid who has everything figured out.

I WRITE MY STORY

But within the emptiness, something ignites.

If his time is limited, he refuses to waste it wallowing. Cam launches a podcast from his hospital bed, transforming his tragedy into truth that cuts straight to the soul. "Time is undefeated," he says, voice unwavering despite everything, "but it can't erase the impact you make."

His words spread like wildfire—not because people pity him, but because he speaks about living with an urgency most people never find. "When it's your time to go, you can't take anything with you," he reminds his growing audience, "but you can leave something behind—if you're intentional."

Cam can't change his diagnosis. But he can choose what to do with the time he has left.

In his final months, he becomes something more powerful than any football player: a voice that reminds people to stop sleepwalking through their own lives.

His legacy isn't defined by the yards he doesn't run or the games he doesn't play.

It's defined by the lives he touches when everything else is stripped away.

Cam proves the most important truth of all: it's not about how long you live—it's about how purposefully you live.

SIQ Tip: I can buy almost anything in life, but I can't buy time. Spend it wisely.

SHIFT HAPPENS

At 24, Evelyn is the young, fierce, unstoppable CEO of a tech startup on the rise in Oakland, CA. She builds her company with sharp instincts, quick decisions, and a vision that never wavers. People admire her for her no-nonsense leadership—especially her two closest friends. To Evelyn, success means moving fast, never second-guessing, and never asking for permission.

But as her company grows, things begin to slip. Product launches miss the mark. Team morale crashes. The drive that once fueled her now feels like it's burning the company down.

Then comes the conference. Evelyn shows up reluctantly, expecting the same recycled advice. But one speaker shatters her expectations: "What if the way you've always done things is limiting you? What if holding so tightly to what you know is blinding you to what you need?"

Those words become an "aha moment" for her. Evelyn has built everything on speed and certainty. But now, she feels the weight of her own limitations. Could she be the problem?

Back in the office, Evelyn takes a risk she's never taken before—she lets go. She walks into the next meeting, looks at her team, and simply asks, "What do you think?"

For the first time, she doesn't drive the conversation—she listens. What follows floors her. Her team lights up, offering fresh ideas and creative solutions she never would've come up with alone. That's when she sees it: her greatest strength isn't making fast decisions—it's knowing when to ask, when to listen, and when to trust.

In just a few months, the company transforms—not because Evelyn has all the answers, but because she opens space for her team to lead too. She realizes that true leadership isn't about being the smartest voice in the room. It's about empowering others to speak up and step in.

In that moment, Evelyn learns her greatest lesson. It's not about running a company—it's about letting go, embracing change, and understanding that real success is built on the strength of those around you.

SIQ Tip: We're quick to laugh at someone who still has an iPhone from 2007, while we hang onto beliefs we've had since 2007. To truly embody my values, remain open to revisiting my opinions. What views have I reconsidered recently?

FACT FALLACY

On a freezing mid-spring night in Indianapolis, IN, the annual city gala is in full swing. The town's elite gather, including Jacob, the city's promising 25-year-old city planner. But the night takes a sharp turn when a priceless, historic vase— symbolic of Indianapolis's architectural legacy—lies shattered on the floor. Whispers ripple through the room, eyes narrowing in on Jacob, who was seen standing closest to the vase just moments before.

"Did you see that? He knocked it over!" someone mutters. Soon, several voices join the chorus.

Jacob, known for his sharp mind and quick decisions, straightens his suit and denies it with icy calm. "I didn't touch the vase," he says, his voice unwavering despite the accusing stares. But the witnesses are adamant. They claim they saw him bump into the display while mingling with officials. His flat-out denial lands as abruptly as the breakage itself.

As the night wears on, Jacob's refusal to acknowledge the incident shifts from puzzling to infuriating. This isn't just any accident—this is Indianapolis's legacy. And he's the city planner—the one responsible for preserving it. Yet here he is, refusing to admit fault, even as evidence and witnesses stack up against him.

The cold outside seeps into the room as tension thickens. Conversations shift from the vase to questions about Jacob's integrity. Is this a sign of something deeper? How can someone in charge of the city's future refuse to admit a simple truth about its past?

In the following days, the community's trust in Jacob collapses. Meetings grow awkward. His once-promising reputation dims. He never confesses. Never apologizes.

And just like that vase, Jacob's credibility shatters—beyond repair.

SIQ Tip: Pretending it never happened doesn't mean it never happened.

GROWTH EXPERIEMNTS

Savannah is trapped in soccer purgatory for eight months.

Every practice, she grinds harder than anyone else. Every drill, she pushes until her lungs burn. But somehow, she's stuck watching teammates who still leave her in the dust. It's like running on a treadmill—exhausting effort with zero progress.

I WRITE MY STORY

The worst part? She used to be the one everyone chased. Now she's the cautionary tale about what happens when natural talent hits its ceiling.

Watching from the sidelines during scrimmages is torture. Players she used to dominate are making moves that seem impossible, playing with a fluidity that makes her feel like she's moving through quicksand.

Then she notices something that breaks her entire understanding of improvement.

The players actually leveling up aren't just training more—they're training different. Bouncing tennis balls off walls while balancing on one foot. Moving through agility cones like they're performing interpretive dance. Working with equipment that looks more like toys than soccer gear.

It looks ridiculous. And that's exactly why Savannah is avoiding it. But desperation has a way of killing pride.

Coach Powell listens to her plea for help with the kind of smile that says he's been waiting for this moment. What happens next breaks down everything she thinks she knows about soccer.

Suddenly, she's training with rubber balls that bounce unpredictably, forcing her brain to recalibrate with every touch. She's doing cognitive puzzles while sprinting until her legs feel like jello. Balance exercises that expose how unstable her "stable" foundation really is.

Every session is a masterclass in humility. Skills she thinks she's mastered crumble under new pressures. Her body rebels against movements that feel completely foreign.

But something unfolds in the chaos. Her brain starts adapting faster. Her first touch becomes surgical and more consistent under pressure. Her decision-making transforms from reactive to proactive. Her body moves with a confidence that surprises even her.

Three weeks later, Savannah isn't just keeping up—she's one of the players setting the pace. The breakthrough isn't about working harder. It's about admitting that her way isn't working and having the courage to look completely foolish while learning a better way.

SIQ Tip: If I want to learn, I have to experiment. I learn by watching and listening: observation and reflection.

MINDFUL WEEDING

Sophia's mind is a war zone, and she's losing.

Every morning, she wakes up to the same vicious whispers: *You're pathetic. You're stupid. No one could ever love someone like you.* The thoughts attack like vultures, circling endlessly until she can barely breathe under their weight.

It's been going on for months. Maybe years. She's lost count.

Her phone becomes her escape—endless scrolling to drown out the noise in her head. But even that stops working. The Instagram posts of happy people feel like personal attacks. The TikToks about self-love sound like cruel jokes.

One afternoon, she's sitting on her bed, tears streaming down her face, when her grandma appears in the doorway. Sophia braces for the usual platitudes—"just think happy thoughts" or "everything happens for a reason"—the kind of advice that makes her want to scream.

Instead, her grandma sits down and says something that stops Sophia cold: "Your mind is like a garden that's been abandoned, honey. Those thoughts? They're weeds. And right now, they're choking out everything good trying to grow."

Something about the metaphor cuts through the years of mental fog. For the first time, Sophia sees her thoughts not as truth, but as intruders she can actually fight.

She starts small. When her brain screams "You're worthless," she imagines yanking that weed out by the roots and planting "I'm learning to see my value." When it hisses "You'll never be enough," she rips it out and plants "I'm enough right now, exactly as I am."

At first, it's brutal. For every weed she pulls, ten more seem to sprout. Her mental garden looks like a disaster zone. But something remarkable happens—she stops being a victim of her own thoughts and becomes their gardener.

Weeks pass. The negative voice doesn't disappear completely, but it gets quieter. Smaller. Less convincing. And for the first time in years, Sophia realizes something that changes everything:

She doesn't have to believe every thought that enters her head. She gets to choose what grows.

SIQ Tip: Negative thoughts are all in the mind. And I can shut that faucet off any time.

TRAINING TRADEOFF

Oliver's been living off his reputation since he was twelve.

"Natural talent." "Soccer prodigy." "The kid who makes it look effortless." In Olympia, these aren't just compliments—they're his entire identity. And honestly? He's addicted to how easy it's always been.

While other players stress about fitness and film study, Oliver coasts on pure ability. Weekends are for Xbox marathons and late-night fast food runs with friends who worship his highlight reels. Training? That's just something he shows up to so coaches don't complain. Then his world implodes in a single sentence.

"U19 National Team scouts will be evaluating players next Tuesday."

Oliver feels sick. For the first time in his life, natural talent feels pathetically small. While he's been treating soccer like a hobby, he knows guys across the state and region have been treating it more serious for a while.

The doubt and panic sets in immediately. What if they're faster? What if they want it more? What if his "effortless" style looks lazy next to players who've been grinding in silence?

So Oliver makes the decision that will haunt him forever: he doesn't show up.

He tells himself he's "not ready yet." That he'll "train harder and try next time." But deep down, he knows the truth—he's terrified of discovering that his natural talent has an expiration date.

Meanwhile, Jax—his less gifted, harder-working teammate—shows up with the confidence of someone who's earned his spot through 6 AM runs and weekend film sessions. The scouts don't just notice Jax. They're mesmerized by him.

Six months later, Oliver gets the text that destroys him: "Jax made the U20 National Team and is going to the U20 World Cup."

Oliver stares at his phone in his childhood bedroom, surrounded by trophies that suddenly feel like participation awards. All those weekends he chose comfort over commitment, all those training sessions he didn't go that hard in, all those moments he thought "natural talent" would save him—they've led to this.

Watching someone else live his dream.

The most talented player in city becomes a cautionary tale about wasted potential. And the worst part? He has no one to blame but the person staring back at him in the mirror.

SIQ Tip: My excuses just gave someone else an opportunity. Listen to that again.

ICE INNOVATIONS

Devin is grinding for two years straight and has absolutely nothing to show for it.

Every practice, he skates until his lungs burn. Every drill, he pushes harder than most. But somehow, he's trapped in this middle ground—working his butt off while watching less dedicated teammates still sail past him toward varsity spots and college scouts.

I WRITE MY STORY

It's maddening. And humiliating.

Then he notices something that challenges his entire perspective for improvement. The players actually improving? They're not on the ice as much. Instead, they're in yoga studios looking like human pretzels. Lifting weights sometimes for reps vs always maxing their weight. Sitting in therapy sessions talking about "mental visualization" like hockey is some kind of meditation retreat.

Devin used to mock this stuff. "Just skate harder," he'd mutter. But "skate harder" is getting him exactly nowhere.

Desperate and out of options, Devin approaches the team's new strength coach—a former Olympic trainer with a reputation for breaking players before rebuilding them into weapons.

She demolishes everything he thinks he knows about improving. Suddenly, Devin's days include explosive plyometrics that leave him feeling the soreness for three days after, yoga sessions that reveal how inflexible his "hockey body" really is, and mental conditioning that exposes his focus like Swiss cheese.

The worst part? Video analysis. Watching himself play in slow-motion HD is psychological torture. Every sloppy turn, every missed opportunity, every fundamental flaw is displayed in brutal clarity. His stickhandling looks like a toddler's. His positioning is chaos disguised as effort.

But here's the plot twist: facing the truth becomes addictive.

Each ugly video session becomes a treasure map of improvement. Each weakness becomes a project. Each failure becomes fuel.

Three months later, Devin doesn't just look different on the ice—he IS different. His movements flow like water. His shots find corners. His reads happen before the play develops.

The kid who used to grind aimlessly? He's now the player everyone studies, trying to decode his transformation.

Turns out the secret isn't working harder. It's working like his weaknesses matter more than his ego.

SIQ Tip: Doing something the way I've always done it, is no justification for continuing to do it (although it may be very tempting to rely on my past).

CLUTCH COMMITMENT

Levi's mouth runs faster than his feet.

Every practice, he delivers Oscar-worthy performances about his "burning desire" to dominate freshman basketball. His teammates can recite his speeches word-for-word: the sacrifice, the dedication, the relentless pursuit of greatness. Even his Instagram bio screams "Built Different 💯🏀."

But watch Levi when the talking stops.

He glides into practice exactly on time—sometimes fashionably late—and becomes a human sprint for the exit when coach blows the whistle. During drills, he perfects the art of looking busy while doing just enough to avoid getting yelled at. His effort has a ceiling: visible enough to avoid drama, lazy enough to preserve energy for his real passion—talking about basketball.

Meanwhile, Marcus operates like a ghost. No speeches. No hashtags. No promises. Just silent, obsessive action that happens in the spaces between everyone else's attention.

5:45 AM: Marcus is alone in the gym, working on the thousand tiny details that separate good from unstoppable.

7:20 PM: Practice ended twenty minutes ago. Marcus is still there, perfecting footwork that will matter in March.

Each day, the gap grows little by little. Marcus's game transforms. His shots start falling more consistently. His defending becomes suffocating and a defining quality. His basketball IQ, recognizing what to do and when to do it, second to none.

When starting lineups are announced, the gym falls silent.

"Starting at point guard... Marcus."

Levi tears up, his shoulders slump. His speeches, his promises, his entire identity—all reduced to expensive air. Coach doesn't even look his direction.

"Real commitment," Coach tells the team, "doesn't announce itself." Basketball, it turns out, is completely deaf to words. It only responds to the language of sweat, repetition, and showing up when the gym is empty and nobody's keeping score.

Levi finally learns the brutal truth: Your mouth can't cash checks your work ethic won't write.

SIQ Tip: Measure commitment by:
- *What time I show up*
- *What time I leave*
- *What I do in the time between.*

Actions always beat words.

TECH TURNAROUND

Justin is the coding prodigy who makes impossible problems look like child's play. For three years, he lives in the fast lane of tech evolution—mastering new frameworks before they become mainstream, solving bugs that make senior developers weep, earning a reputation as the guy who can fix anything.

Then the fire just... dies. Suddenly, opening his laptop feels like a chore. New programming languages look boring. The cutting-edge projects that used to keep him up at night now feel like obligations. He convinces himself he's hit his ceiling—that maybe he isn't as brilliant as everyone thinks.

The truth is far more devastating.

At a mandatory company workshop, Justin sits in a sterile conference room, half-listening to speakers speak about staying curious. But one phrase cuts through his mental fog like a knife: "The moment you stop being uncomfortable, you stop growing."

He hasn't reached his limit. He's just been hiding from discomfort for so long that his brain goes to sleep.

For months, he has been coasting on skills he mastered years ago, avoiding anything that might make him feel stupid or confused. While the tech world sprints forward, he plants himself in a comfort zone and calls it expertise.

That night, Justin does something uncomfortable—he signs up for a machine learning course that makes him feel like a complete beginner. He joins coding meetups where half the conversations go over his head. He downloads tools that frustrate him more than they excite him.

It's brutal. His ego gets destroyed on a regular basis. But something noticeable happens in the struggle. The curiosity that made him great starts flickering back to life. Late nights become adventures again instead of obligations. Problems become puzzles instead of burdens.

Within three months, Justin isn't just coding again—he is innovating. New opportunities flood in. His career trajectory explodes. He uncovers something important: You don't stop learning because you've reached your limit. You stop learning because you've gotten too comfortable to keep climbing.

And comfort is the silent killer of greatness.

SIQ Tip: I do not stop learning and improving because I have reached some innate limit on my performance. I stop learning and improving because I'm no longer as engaged in developing the skillsets I once was.

CRUMBY IDEAS
On a freezing winter morning, 14-year-old Sara drags herself to a local youth business seminar, her curiosity stronger than her desire to stay in bed. The community center is packed with teenagers who look just as tired as she does.

I WRITE MY STORY

But when a young, charismatic CEO takes the stage, everything changes. He shares a story—epic failures, unexpected breakthroughs, and lessons that cost him everything to learn. Sara hangs on every word.

After the seminar, she approaches him with the kind of nervous energy that comes from meeting someone who's actually living her dream. He smiles and tells her something that sticks with her forever: "Every path to success leaves clues. If you pay close attention, you'll find strategies and habits that can guide you. Collect as many of those as you can."

It's the kind of advice that rewires your thinking. Sara has always loved baking—her chocolate chip cookies are legendary among her friends—but she's never thought of it as anything more than a hobby. That night, she decides to turn her passion into something real.

Throughout the brutal winter months, Sara becomes a kind of detective, studying successful bakeries, having conversations, and seeing how she can make the ideas her own. She follows their Instagram feeds, researches their origin stories, and notes what makes customers obsess over certain options and brands.

She practices relentlessly in her kitchen, perfecting three show-stopping cookie recipes that make her family beg for more.

Using clues she discovers—distinctive branding, obsessive quality control, and genuine community connection—Sara launches "Sara's Sweet Secrets." Her small online business explodes locally, with customers raving about both her incredible cookies and her creative social media presence.

At school events and community fairs, Sara shares her journey, encouraging others to find their own "success crumbs." She proves that even at 14, with the right mindset and intentional action, you can turn passion into profit.

SIQ Tip: Success leaves crumbs... how many can I find? Once I find them, apply them!

DISTRACTED MASTERY

Asher lives and breathes violin, dreaming of performing on stages most musicians only see on TV or in magazines. But despite his burning passion for music, distractions are absolutely destroying his progress.

His phone buzzes nonstop with notifications, friends constantly have "epic" plans that sound way more fun than practice, and the endless scroll of TikTok and Instagram sucks away hours that should be spent perfecting his craft.

Everything changes at a masterclass. The instructor's words about discipline and focus cut through all his excuses: "Talent without focus is just potential. And potential doesn't get you on stage."

That night, Asher makes a decision that feels both terrifying and liberating: no more letting distractions control his future. He creates a strict practice schedule, puts his phone in another room during sessions, and tells his friends he's only available on weekends.

It doesn't take long for things to come together. His violin becomes an extension of his soul. Each note flows with depth and clarity he's never experienced before. Hours of uninterrupted practice turn into days, then weeks of the most productive music-making of his life. His confidence explodes as he sees and feels himself actually improving instead of just going through the motions.

Months later, Asher stands before the audition panel of the city's most prestigious youth orchestra, his heart pounding. When he starts playing, everything else disappears. Every sacrifice, every declined invitation, every hour of disciplined practice pours through his fingers.

When the phone rings two weeks later with his acceptance, Asher realizes the most important lesson of his musical journey: Mastering his craft isn't just about practicing harder—it's about protecting his dreams from a world designed to distract him.

SIQ Tip: The biggest obstacle to my mastery isn't mediocrity; it's my distractions.

PRESSURE PUSH

On a mild winter afternoon in Boston, 17-year-old Hudson is obsessed with one goal: making the varsity lacrosse team. The high school team has a storied program, ranked nationally in the top 10 for years.

Hudson loves messing around in casual scrimmages with friends, but when it comes to pushing himself beyond his comfort zone? Not so much. His skills have completely plateaued, and deep down, he knows he's holding himself back.

Everything shifts when Coach Clarke announces varsity tryouts with brutal honesty: "There are only twelve spots available. May the best players earn 'em."

I WRITE MY STORY

Suddenly, Hudson feels the crushing weight of pressure—but also something unexpected. He feels alive.

With limited time and everything on the line, Hudson commits to a tweaked approach. Instead of casual weekend pickup games, he starts grinding daily, waking up at 5 a.m. to train before school. Taking advantage of the unusually mild winter weather, he trains outdoors more than ever.

Hudson works obsessively to perfect his stick handling, drilling the same moves until they become instinctive. He spends hours improving shooting off-balance and in tight spaces, aiming for specific spots over and over. His physical conditioning goes from adequate to beast mode.

During the two weeks of tryouts, Hudson is still nervous—but excited. The pressure unlocks something inside him he didn't expect. As he competes, his passes are crisp and quick, his elusiveness and dodging confident, and he's locked in mentally.

Hudson surprises everyone, including himself, with the consistent quality play he brings each day.

When the roster goes up, Hudson's name is on it.

Reading that list, Hudson realizes pressure isn't his enemy—it's his instigator. Casual play was fun, but embracing real challenges with everything on the line is what finally elevates his game to another level.

SIQ Tip: With the absence of pressure, it's hard to do great things.

RICH RELAXATION

Growing up in Vermont, 20-year-old Eli watches everyone around him chase the same dream: more money, bigger houses, nicer cars. His parents, neighbors, even his college friends are obsessed with climbing the financial ladder, convinced that wealth means having more stuff than everyone else.

So Eli does what he thinks he's supposed to do after college. He lands a high-paying corporate job, works insane hours, and saves every penny he can. On paper, he's winning. In reality, he feels completely empty.

His life becomes a soul-crushing cycle: work, eat, sleep, repeat. No time for hobbies, relationships, or anything that actually matters to him. He's making money but losing himself in the process.

Everything starts to shift on a random summer night when he reconnects with his old friend Nate, who runs a small outdoor adventure company. Nate isn't rich by society's standards, but something about him is different—lighter, happier, more alive.

Over a couple drinks at a local dive bar, Eli vents about feeling trapped despite his financial success. Nate listens, then drops an idea that shatters Eli's perspective:

"Dude, wealth isn't about how much money you have. It's about having the freedom and time to do more of what you actually love with people you like."

Eli suddenly sees everything through a new lens. So simple, but so true.

Nate spends his days leading hiking trips, traveling to incredible places, and building genuine relationships with people who share his interests. He isn't wealthy in dollars, but he's rich in time and experience.

That conversation rewires Eli's brain. He starts questioning everything: Why is he sacrificing his life for a bank account? What's the point of financial security if he's too miserable and busy to enjoy it?

Eli begins to restructure his priorities, focusing on gaining control over his time rather than just collecting money. He realizes that real wealth is the freedom to live life on his own terms.

SIQ Tip: Those that told me wealth is about having more money than anyone else, lied. Wealth is about having more freedom of time than anyone else.

FLAW FORWARD

Harper is incredibly talented at 23, but she has a devastating problem: she never finishes anything. Her studio is a graveyard of half-completed paintings, each one abandoned the moment she spots the tiniest flaw.

Every time Harper gets close to finishing a piece, she picks it apart. "That shadow is slightly off." "The proportions aren't exactly right." "A real artist would never make this mistake."

So, she starts over. And over. And over.

Her canvases pile up like broken dreams—unfinished and untouched—while Harper's confidence slowly crumbles.

I WRITE MY STORY

She's stuck in an endless cycle of starting but never completing, creating but never sharing.

One afternoon, her art mentor finds her staring at yet another abandoned painting, tears of frustration in her eyes.

"Perfectionism is a prison, Harper," she says gently. "It's not protecting your art—it's killing it. Stop chasing perfection and start chasing progress. Make each piece better than the last one, not better than some impossible standard."

Harper wants to argue, but deep down she knows her mentor is right. Reluctantly, she tries a different approach.

Instead of aiming for flawless, Harper aims for finished. She forces herself to accept that her work doesn't need to be perfect—just better than her previous attempt. When she catches herself obsessing over tiny details, she pushes through and keeps painting.

And then something crazy happens. Her colors become bolder because she's not afraid of making mistakes. Her brushstrokes grow more confident because she stops second-guessing every movement.

Within months, Harper's studio walls are covered with completed paintings. Each one tells the story of her growth— her willingness to embrace imperfection, her journey from paralyzed perfectionist to productive artist.

Harper finally understands: perfectionism keeps her frozen, but progress sets her free.

SIQ Tip: *People are crippled by perfection. Just keep moving forward - improvement is the goal, not perfection.*

OPTIONS OPEN

On a surprisingly mild winter day in Nebraska, 24-year-old Violet feels suffocated by her small town's obsession with forcing people into boxes. Everyone believes life is all about choosing sides—you can be successful OR happy, wealthy OR kind, creative OR practical. Every decision feels like a fork in the road designed to limit what's possible.

But Violet refuses to live within those suffocating boundaries.

She's obsessed with both digital art and computer science. She loves playing volleyball and reading. When people tell her to "pick a lane" and focus on just one thing, Violet chooses rebellion. She believes life doesn't have to be either/or—it can be both/and.

Her friends think she's crazy. "You can't be good at everything," they say. "You need to specialize if you want to succeed."

Violet challenges that belief. As she gets older, her unique approach becomes her superpower. She pursues a career in UX design, perfectly blending her artistic creativity with technical problem-solving skills. Her diverse interests don't make her scattered—they make her irreplaceable.

Her life becomes a masterpiece of integration. She codes beautiful apps by day, paints murals on weekends, plays in a volleyball league, and leads philosophy discussion groups at the local library. Success and fulfillment aren't competing—they amplify each other.

Soon, Violet's approach starts inspiring others in her conservative town. Watching her live out both her passions and her principles, many begin questioning their own self-imposed limitations. Why can't they be both ambitious AND kind? Why can't they pursue financial success AND creative fulfillment?

Violet's example opens their eyes to life's endless possibilities. She shows them that the richest, most meaningful things come from embracing multiple passions instead of limiting themselves to artificial categories.

Her small Nebraska town slowly transforms as more people choose "and" over "or," discovering that the most extraordinary lives are built by refusing to choose between the things that make them come alive.

SIQ Tip: Society is obsessed with 'or'. Challenge myself to be obsessed with 'and'!

FUTURE FORMING
At 21, Leo feels like a complete failure. He's switched majors three times, tried everything from photography to coding to marine biology, and is seriously considering dropping out of college altogether. While everyone around him seems to have their lives figured out, Leo feels lost—watching his friends move forward while he spins his wheels.

The pressure is crushing. His parents keep asking about his "plan," professors question his commitment, and social media is filled with peers landing internships and celebrating achievements. Leo feels like he's falling further behind every day.

One freezing winter evening, feeling especially stuck as the holidays approach, Leo drives to his grandpa's house. His grandpa has always been his hero—a guy who's lived a thousand lives, traveled the world, and somehow makes everything look effortless.

Sitting by the crackling fire in his grandpa's living room, Leo finally breaks down. "Grandpa, I'm completely lost. Everyone else knows exactly what they're doing, and I feel like I'm wasting my life trying random stuff that leads nowhere."

His grandpa listens carefully, then smiles in that gentle way that always makes Leo feel understood.

"Leo," he says softly, "you're not lost—you're just starting your real journey. At your age, I had zero clue where life was taking me. I thought I'd be a farmer, then tried being a mechanic, ended up in the military, and somehow became a teacher. Life's path isn't a straight line, kiddo. Every twist and turn teaches you something you'll need later."

It doesn't just register—it resonates. Suddenly, Leo's explorations and experiments don't seem like signs of failure—they're signs of curiosity, courage, and growth. He's not behind; he's gathering experiences, building a unique foundation that will serve him in ways he can't even imagine yet.

From that point on, Leo embraces his uncertainty as part of the adventure, trusting every confusing step is guiding him exactly where he needs to be.

SIQ Tip: I'm not lost. I'm just early in the process.

MATCH MINDSET

On a chilly Florida evening, Grayson stands alone on the tennis court, his racket feeling heavier than usual. He's always loved tennis, dreaming of winning tournaments and holding trophies high. But lately, every jump in competition feels like a guaranteed beatdown from players way ahead of him.

Each loss hits hard. His confidence starts slipping, and after another rough match where he barely wins three games, Grayson seriously thinks about quitting.

Coach Taylor finds him sitting on the bench afterward, steam rising in the cold air. "Listen," Coach says gently, "success isn't about winning every match. It's about showing up after. Real champions—the ones who not only get to the top but stay there—they show up. Especially after losses. They're ready to go again."

Those words land harder than expected. Grayson realizes it's not losing he fears—it's not knowing if he can keep getting back up when his confidence takes another hit.

Something shifts that night. Grayson makes a quiet decision: he won't let setbacks write his story. He's going to keep showing up. The very next morning, he's back on the court, racket in hand, ready to face whatever the day throws at him.

He still loses matches, but he stops seeing losses simply as failure. Instead, they become data. What needs work? What clicked? How can he adjust? Every match turns into a lesson.

He focuses on small, controllable details and leans into the discomfort of leveling up. His technique sharpens. His mental toughness becomes a weapon to help him, not work against him. The habit he becomes obsessed with, showing up.

Over the semester, something changes inside Grayson. Winning every match isn't the goal anymore—getting better is. He starts celebrating the little wins that are measurable: completing more of his first serves, quicker and more confident footwork he can evaluate through video, and improving his backhand returns after the first set, as he starts getting more fatigued.

Florida's brutal spring doesn't shake him. Every time Grayson steps onto the court—win or lose—he stands taller. More confident. More committed. He finally understands the bigger picture: success doesn't mean avoiding failure. It means being brave enough to keep showing up when every part of you wants to walk away.

SIQ Tip: Success isn't winning; success is getting back up after I've been pushed down. Over. And over. And over.

PART 2

THE EMOTIONAL ROLLERCOASTER

THE EMOTIONAL ROLLERCOASTER

As a young adult, you're facing mental health challenges no generation has encountered prior: the pressure to be perfect while scrolling through curated lives, the feeling of isolation despite being hyper-connected, and feeling a sense of impostor syndrome that whispers "you're not enough," even when breaking barriers.

Every day you don't develop emotional resilience, anxiety gets stronger. Every moment you avoid building authentic confidence by keeping the promises you tell yourself, self-doubt digs deeper roots.

But here's what nobody reminds you of: the same mental skills that save elite athletes and create breakthrough innovations can transform your daily experience. The difference between those who thrive and those who barely survive isn't talent or luck—it's mastering the mental game.

The stories you're about to read are examples for you to learn from, relate to and use as a reference to help guide you through your personal emotional situations. Each character faces the exact struggles you're navigating: crushing expectations, fearing failure, perfectionism, or searching for authentic connection in a digital world.

The cost of ignoring these skills, isn't just struggling—it's watching your future self slip away while others who improve their mental skills soar past you. Your mental health isn't about surviving anymore: it's about building and sustaining the good life you deserve.

The choice is yours, but the window won't stay open forever. I again conclude each story with one SIQ Tip (simple, immediate, quick) to challenge you to live an even better life, sooner.

EMOTIONAL EQUATION

Abby always believes her intelligence defines her. At 19, she aces every class and is the person everyone turns to for advice. But during a heated argument with her best friend, Abby completely loses control. Her words embarrass and hurt someone she says she truly cares about—and it makes her painfully aware that intellect alone isn't enough.

Later that evening, her phone rings. It's her older cousin, a young psychologist she's always admired. As they catch up, Abby shares what happened.

"Abby," he asks gently, "do you want me to just listen or share some advice?" "Some advice would be nice," she says quietly. "Being smart is important, but your emotional intelligence shapes your relationships. Recognizing and managing your emotions is essential—because if you don't, they'll control you. And when that happens, you're usually left with embarrassment and regret. That's the tradeoff. And remember—it's your choice."

Abby thinks about what he says. She starts observing her reactions more carefully. Over time, she learns to pause, breathe, and respond more thoughtfully instead of impulsively lashing out. Her relationships start improving more than she expects, and she feels genuinely in control. She's finally cracking the code of emotional intelligence—but this is just the beginning.

As Abby begins to feel more balanced, we shift to Ethan. At 17, he's on the verge of making a critical mistake—all because his temporary emotions are clouding his judgment.

THE EMOTIONAL ROLLERCOASTER

SIQ Tip: Be aware of my emotions. Just as important, knowing how to control them is one of the most important skills I'll ever learn, for anything.

FRUSTRATION FIX

Ethan slams his bedroom door, frustration running through him. At 17, anger is his default response—school stress, fading friendships, nonstop arguments. He feels stuck in a cycle he can't break.

When Maya, his older sister, knocks softly and steps in, she sees through everything. She's been there before. Sitting beside him, she says gently, "Ethan, I've been where you are. But you've got to ask yourself—what's really behind all that anger? What's triggering it?"

He wants to shrug her off, but something in her tone makes him pause. Slowly, he admits what he's been hiding: beneath the anger is fear—fear of failing, fear of being left out, fear of ending up alone.

Maya helps him unpack it all. She teaches him how to notice his emotional patterns, how to pause in the heat of the moment, breathe, and ask himself what he's really feeling. Instead of exploding, he starts identifying his real emotions before they take over.

His biggest breakthrough? Mapping his triggers. He realizes the same things set him off over and over—getting a graded test back, seeing friends hang out without him, feeling swamped by schoolwork. Now, he sees them not as enemies, but as signals—reminders to check in with himself.

Over the next few weeks, Ethan keeps practicing. The more he names his triggers, the less control they have. His reactions get slower, more thoughtful. His relationships start healing.

Ethan learns that emotional awareness is a skill. His emotions aren't problems—they're messages. And now, he's finally listening.

Just as Ethan finds balance, we shift to Alyssa. She's 24, finally working her dream job—but her emotional outbursts are putting everything on the line. She's never learned to manage stress, and now, it's threatening to cost her everything.

SIQ Tip: Reflect on what it is that triggers me. Only then can I recognize it, pause it, and change it. Be on purpose.

SUCCESSFUL SETBACKS

Alyssa is driven. At 24, she lands her dream job at a top-tier marketing firm and quickly rises through the ranks with bold ideas and nonstop work ethic.

Success comes fast. Recognition, praise—it all feels like validation. But before long, things start shifting. Deadlines that once excited her now feel suffocating. Meetings that used to energize her leave her agitated and impatient.

The pressure of staying at the top begins to crack her calm. She doesn't want to admit it, but her emotions start steering her reactions. After one especially tense meeting ends with her snapping at a colleague, Candy pulls her aside.

"Alyssa," Candy says gently, "success can sneak up on you. When you're comfortable, it's easy to stop growing. The way you've been reacting lately? That's not you—it's a sign something deeper is off. You can't control everything, but you can always control how you respond."

Alyssa bristles at first. But then Candy adds, "Next time you feel that frustration build, pause and breathe. Ask yourself— what's really behind it? Fear? Pressure? Burnout?"

That conversation changes everything. Alyssa starts tracking her emotional patterns. She notices certain triggers—when project plans suddenly shift, when her ideas are questioned, when she feels like she's pulling more weight than her team. These moments fuel her outbursts.

But now she sees them coming. In her next high-pressure meeting, the old frustration rises—but instead of reacting, she pauses. Breathes. Asks herself what's actually happening underneath the irritation.

Her self-awareness gives her control. She stops fighting her emotions and starts guiding them. Her responses become thoughtful instead of reactive. She sees that managing success isn't just about results—it's about mindset.

And just as Alyssa finds her emotional balance, we meet Ryan—a 14-year-old soccer prodigy competing with the Philadelphia Union's MLS Next team. He's already building the kind of emotional skills most adults haven't even started learning.

SIQ Tip: When I find myself experiencing wins, the most important thing I can do is continue showing up, continue to look for small ways to improve and continue to add skills for my future self.

THE EMOTIONAL ROLLERCOASTER

TACKLING TENSION

Ryan stands at center line, eyes scanning the field under the blinding stadium lights. At 14, he's the youngest player on the U17 Philadelphia Union, but his composure matches the oldest players on the pitch. Tonight, they're up against their most physical rivals—NYCFC. The air is muggy and thick, sweat already dripping before the whistle even blows.

As adrenaline surges through his body, Ryan remembers his coach's words. He closes his eyes and takes a slow breath— in for four seconds, out for four. He does it again. And again. The tension in his hands and shoulders eases. He's grounded now. Ready.

Within five minutes, he intercepts a pass, slips the ball through a defender's legs, and delivers a perfectly weighted assist with the outside of his right foot. Boom—opening goal.

The game grows more physical as time ticks on. Late in the second half, with the score knotted at 2-2, Ryan gets taken out just outside the box. His ankle is bleeding. He stays down, breathing fast and shallow, emotions flaring.

But instead of losing control, Ryan closes his eyes, returns to his breath, and regains his focus. He stands, walks to the ball, shakes out his hands, and pictures exactly where he wants to place the shot.

The ref blows the whistle. One final inhale. One solid strike. The ball sails over the wall, kisses the bottom of the crossbar, and bounces in—game-winner.

The stadium erupts. His teammates storm him, shouting with joy as the crowd roars behind them.

THE EMOTIONAL ROLLERCOASTER

In the middle of the celebration, Ryan catches sight of a familiar face in the stands—Grace, a 19-year-old college student he recently met at a sports psych workshop. She once shared with him how anger had derailed her high school athletic career. Tonight, she watches a younger player win with a calm demeanor she never mastered—yet.

SIQ Tip: Understanding how to manage stressful situations and using breathing techniques to relax tension in my hands, feet, shoulders and other areas will allow me to optimize my performances.

RAGE RELEASE

Grace's thumb flies across her phone screen, jaw clenched as she watches Ashley's stories. A fresh subtweet from someone in her friend group makes every notification sting. Her reflection scowls back at her through the glass as she doom-scrolls, feeding the fire.

Tony notices her white-knuckled grip. "You've been glaring at that thing for an hour," he says, flopping onto the couch. "Staying mad is like keeping a toxic app—drains your battery, wrecks your vibe."

Grace glances up. She's just wasted her entire evening on drama that probably won't matter by next week.

"When someone makes you mad, they're living rent-free in your head," Tony adds. "Why give them the keys?"

Later in her room, Grace tries something new—phone down, deep breaths. She imagines her anger as a notification she can swipe away. The knot in her chest begins to loosen.

THE EMOTIONAL ROLLERCOASTER

The next day at school, she doesn't ice Ashley out. She doesn't stir the pot. She just stays neutral. Not fake—just grounded. The drama fizzles before it can catch fire. By lunch, she's dodged a whole day of emotional wreckage.

By sixth period, she catches herself smiling. Not the kind you force to keep up appearances—the kind that sneaks out when you forget to be mad. She even laughs at something Mr. Olson says. A real laugh.

While packing up, she finds a note tucked into her binder. Just three words. No name: *Thanks for today.* Her brow furrows. No clue who wrote it—but somehow, she doesn't need to know. It's enough to remind her: people notice when you stop throwing wood on the fire.

As she heads to her next class, Grace spots Samantha sitting alone at their usual lunch table, picking at her food with that same distant stare she's worn for weeks. Grace has just learned to let go of today's drama—but she wonders if Samantha's still stuck inside yesterday's situation.

SIQ Tip: When I experience anger, pause and ask: "Is this worth my energy?" Then breathe, step back, and choose my response instead of automatically reacting. My peace of mind is too valuable to let someone else's actions steal it.

REFRAMING REGRET

Samantha, a 16-year-old with a shy demeanor, sits quietly in the back of her classroom, her mind swimming with memories of missed opportunities. Each memory burns with the sharp pain of regret—school dances she's skipped, her opinions never shared to help someone, all because of the haunting fear of repeating past embarrassments. But a recent conversation with her older brother is sparking a shift in her perspective.

"Regret is a challenging feeling to deal with," he tells her. "Use it as fuel for your next situation. It's the only way to move past it. Ask yourself, 'how will I feel about it tomorrow,' if you don't do something." His words echo in her mind as she listens to her classmates laugh and share stories from their recent weekends.

Today, Samantha decides, will be different. She's signing up for the school play auditions—a thought that would have horrified her just a week ago. Her heart pounds as she approaches the sign-up sheet, her hand trembling slightly as she writes her name. She knows her brother is right: the regret of not trying will hurt more than potential embarrassment.

As she recites her lines during auditions, feeling an unexpected thrill of the spotlight warming her face, she realizes that the stage isn't as intimidating as she's made it out to be. Her voice grows stronger with each word, and for the first time in months, she feels truly alive. The other students watch with genuine interest, not the judgment she'd imagined. In the end, she's proud that she's chosen to transform her regret into a stepping stone.

As she steps off the stage, feeling a new sense of confidence, her story of overcoming fear begins spreading throughout the school. Students who've watched her transformation are encouraged by her decision. Her drama teacher approaches with a smile, commenting on her natural stage presence.

Not too far from where Samantha lives is a 21-year-old college student named Finn. He feels held back by a similar fear of embarrassment and rarely contributes in his classes because of what others might say and think. But today, as word of Samantha's brave audition reaches him through mutual friends, something makes him wonder if he can grow past his self-imposed limitations.

SIQ Tip: Use regret to fuel me to do more, not hold me back and do less.

ESCAPE EMBARRASSMENT
Finn, a 21-year-old college student, is quietly intelligent but overwhelmingly silenced by his fear of embarrassment. This anxiety stymies his potential, locking his insights and contributions away during class discussions, where the specter of judgment feels overbearing. But everything changes when he stumbles upon a podcast episode a friend shares with him.

The host talks about embarrassment not as a dead-end, but as a detour on the path to growth. The podcaster's candid stories about learning from, rather than being defined by mistakes, resonate deeply with Finn. It's a perspective shift that shines a light on a potential new path forward. He finds himself replaying the episode, absorbing the host's message that courage isn't the absence of fear—it's action despite fear.

The very next day, Finn hesitates only briefly before raising his hand in a crowded lecture hall. His palm is sweaty as he grips his pen, and his heart races as the professor calls on him. But with each word he speaks, his fear diminishes more and more. His classmates respond positively, nodding and engaging with his ideas, further validating his newfound courage and input.

THE EMOTIONAL ROLLERCOASTER

So Finn begins to participate more regularly, each contribution easing his fear of judgment a little more. He discovers that most students are too focused on their own insecurities to judge him harshly. He even joins a campus club, speaking up in small group settings, discovering that vulnerability inspires connection rather than ridicule. His ideas spark meaningful discussions, and more students start approaching him after class to continue conversations.

Finn has finally learned to channel his fear into a force for personal evolution. He's transforming from a silent observer into an active participant in his own education.

Meanwhile, 15-year-old Avery, an optimist through and through, faces her own challenge: growing up with pessimistic parents. Despite their gloomy outlook, Avery's relentless positivity has always been her shield. But lately, she finds herself second-guessing her optimism, especially when dinner conversations end in uncomfortable silence, her hopeful observations absorbed without acknowledgment. Avery wonders if positivity really is enough to change her surroundings, or if she's just naive to keep trying.

SIQ Tip: Embarrassment is made up and is a limiting belief that will only keep me from doing more.

POSITIVITY PLAYER
Avery, a 15-year-old multi-sport athlete playing field hockey, basketball, and volleyball, is a beacon of positivity. But her parents often cast shadows of doubt and pessimism around her bright energy. They worry constantly about the risks of sports injuries, the pressures of competition, and the likelihood of disappointment, but Avery refuses to let their fears dim her bright outlook.

THE EMOTIONAL ROLLERCOASTER

One rainy evening, after a particularly challenging volleyball match that's going into overtime, Avery's team faces a big deficit. Her parents, watching from the bleachers, mutter about the inevitable loss with a couple other parents, their voices carrying that familiar tone of resigned defeat. But Avery continues to radiate optimism, attempting to rally her teammates as sweat drips down her face and the scoreboard glares ominously.

"Keep chipping away! We've got this," she cheers, her voice ringing clear in the damp gym air. Her teammates look exhausted, but something about her infectious confidence sparks new energy in their tired limbs. She's clapping her hands, calling out encouragement, refusing to acknowledge the possibility of defeat even as the clock ticks down.

With her unwavering belief pushing them, she leads a stunning comeback, her team scoring point after crucial point. The gym erupts as they clinch the win in the final moments, and Avery's teammates swarm her in celebration. She's beaming, not just from victory, but from proving once again that hope isn't naive—it's powerful.

As they drive home, her parents sit unusually quiet, the glow of streetlights flickering across their thoughtful faces. The silence stretches, heavy with unspoken realizations. Finally, her mom turns to her, a genuine smile breaking through years of practiced skepticism. "Maybe you're right, Avery. Sometimes, things really do work out for the better."

Avery's consistent optimism has not only lifted her team but is beginning to transform her parents' entire outlook on life. She's proving that positivity isn't just feel-good fluff—it's a force that creates real change.

Meanwhile, in Buffalo, NY, 23-year-old Logan grapples with his own challenges on a warm May evening. As a medical student, he's consumed by a relentless pursuit of popularity among his peers and professors, believing it's crucial for his future success.

SIQ Tip: Optimism is a key ingredient to accomplishing anything. It will help turn my possibilities into probabilities.

PAST PRISON

On a warm May evening in Buffalo, Logan, a 23-year-old medical student, finds himself tangled in a web of his own ambition. Driven and competitive, Logan has long convinced himself that popularity among peers is vital to his future success. He spends countless hours networking, schmoozing with professors, and calculating every interaction for maximum social advantage. But a single conversation with an older medical mentor is beginning to challenge that assumption.

After quietly observing Logan's exhausting performance for weeks, his mentor—a seasoned physician with kind but knowing eyes—finally speaks up. "Logan, maybe instead of chasing popularity and recognition, you should aim for meaningful wins each day." The words hit Logan like a diagnosis he wasn't expecting but desperately needed to hear.

Logan starts questioning whether his relentless pursuit of peer approval is truly rewarding, or simply draining the life out of him. He notices how hollow he feels after each networking event, how his relationships feel transactional rather than genuine. He decides it's time for a change, focusing more on his personal growth and genuine impact rather than social climbing.

THE EMOTIONAL ROLLERCOASTER

Logan begins volunteering at a local clinic, where subtle but powerful interactions quickly reshape his perspective. Teaching a worried patient about their medication, bringing clarity to someone's health concerns, or simply offering empathy during a difficult diagnosis—each interaction feels profoundly rewarding, far outweighing the temporary thrill of academic praise or professional recognition.

To Logan's surprise, his new approach brings him a deeper sense of accomplishment—and genuine respect from his peers that he never had to chase. By prioritizing meaningful connections and authentic care over calculated networking, respect comes naturally rather than as something he has to desperately pursue through exhausting social maneuvering.

Logan learns that true fulfillment isn't found in public acknowledgment but in quiet moments of impact—helping someone in ways they'll always remember, making a difference that matters beyond any grade or accolade.

Logan's journey is unique, but elsewhere, 18-year-old Natalie, from Mississippi, wrestles with her own inner demons. Consumed by shame from past mistakes, she struggles to move forward, her life overshadowed by decisions she can't change and regrets that seem to follow her everywhere she goes.

SIQ Tip: It's not about how high I go but how far I've come. It's not about experiencing the best moment (it's short-lived) but experiencing more wins.

SHEDDING SHAME

On a scorching Mississippi summer day, 18-year-old Natalie feels trapped by shadows from past mistakes, each regret gripping her tighter than the last. Mornings feel suffocating, the weight of shame pressing on her chest, making each step forward feel impossible.

Her friends notice her slipping away—ignoring texts, dodging calls, quietly vanishing from their lives. Finally, Erika, her closest friend, has enough and decides to step in.

Under the sprawling branches of an old oak tree, Erika gently confronts Natalie. Sharing something she recently read, Erika says, "What if instead of punishing yourself endlessly, you accepted what happened, forgave yourself for being human, and let it fuel your growth rather than stunt it?"

Natalie sits in silence, stunned. Erika's words break through the layers of shame she's grown used to. Slowly, a new path begins forming in her mind—a way forward that doesn't involve drowning in regret, but rising above it.

Natalie chooses to gradually reconnect with her community. She starts volunteering at local crisis centers, channeling her experiences into meaningful support for others facing their darkest moments. What once feels like unbearable shame becomes her most powerful strength: genuine empathy born from personal understanding.

Her story becomes proof that you can rise from a low point, transforming personal anguish into healing—for yourself and those around you.

Meanwhile, across the country, 19-year-old Gabriel is facing his own battle. He feels like a walking disaster magnet, constantly getting hit with one blow after another. The universe seems determined to crush him from every possible angle—or at least that's how it feels.

THE EMOTIONAL ROLLERCOASTER

*SIQ Tip: Let go of my past mistakes and forgive myself.
Define my moments, don't let my moments define me.*

PIVOT POINT

Nineteen-year-old Gabriel always feels like he's a magnet for
misfortune, absorbing the worst from every situation in his
small Oregon town. Whether it's school troubles, family
disputes, or just daily disappointments, Gabriel finds himself
constantly questioning, "Why does everything bad happen to
me?" The relentless strain clouds his view of life, painting his
days in persistent shades of gray that seem impossible to
escape.

One rainy afternoon, as Gabriel tucks himself into the quiet
corners of the local library seeking refuge from another
difficult day, he stumbles upon a book that challenges his
entire perception. The author speaks of life's proximity to
change, emphasizing how just one decision or conversation
can pivot someone's path toward something entirely new. The
concept feels foreign but intriguing—the idea that he might
have more control than he thinks.

Curious and desperate for anything different, Gabriel begins
to internalize the idea, consciously shifting his mindset from
one of victimhood to one of potential. It's not easy; years of
negative thinking don't disappear overnight. But he starts
small, catching himself when he spirals into "why me"
thinking and asking instead, "what can I do about this?"

Gabriel makes a conscious decision to change his approach at
school. He starts participating more in class discussions,
raising his hand even when he's not completely confident, and
seeking solutions rather than dwelling endlessly on problems.
Slowly, his days begin to brighten as he notices small

victories accumulating—a teacher's encouraging nod, a successful presentation, a homework assignment completed without drama—reinforcing his new belief in the power of one good decision.

One of the most surprising outcomes is that a few more classmates become willing to engage with him, not just in class but outside of it. They invite him to study groups and weekend hangouts, drawn to his newfound energy and problem-solving attitude rather than repelled by constant negativity.

This shift takes us to Southern California, where 17-year-old Brooklyn, known for her insightful nature and remarkable maturity, navigates her own challenges. As captain of her ECNL soccer team, she recognizes that her teammates respond not just to her good intentions but to her concrete actions. She's quickly becoming a pivotal figure both on and off the field.

SIQ Tip: I'm one decision away from changing the rest of my life - always.

SOCCER STAMINA
In the warm glow of a Southern California sunset, 17-year-old Brooklyn stands at the center of the field, her team huddled around her. As captain of her ECNL soccer team, she leads with quiet confidence, knowing her actions speak louder than her words. Today is their biggest match of the season—a game that could lock in first place with just four games to go before playoffs.

Despite Brooklyn's steady performance and dominant play, the game slips away, moment by moment, until the final whistle blows. The loss stings, but Brooklyn knows this moment will define something bigger.

She gathers her team, voice calm and composed despite the disappointment. "This loss doesn't define us or our season," she tells them. "Our response does. Let's make sure we influence tomorrow, and that starts with what we do tonight. Get some rest. Come ready to work."

The next morning, Brooklyn is the first one on the field. Dew still clings to the grass as she runs conditioning drills and works through finishing reps before anyone else arrives. Her energy sets the tone. Soon the entire team is flying through practice—pushing harder, staying sharper, raising their level.

The season builds into the playoffs. They go on a tear, proving themselves as a national powerhouse. But it's not just the wins that shift—it's the mindset. That moment after the loss becomes the spark.

Her teammates realize leadership isn't about being perfect. It's about what you do when things fall apart. It's about showing up the next day anyway—especially when it's hard.

As Brooklyn's story of resilience unfolds on the West Coast, Felipe—a 17-year-old from New York—faces his own leadership challenge: one that starts at home with a younger brother who watches his every move.

SIQ Tip: Intentions are measured on the inside; actions are measured on the outside.

PROACTIVE PITCH

In the bustling heart of New York City, 17-year-old Felipe moves with purpose, his proactive personality clear in everything he does. Known among his peers for always stepping up, Felipe takes his role as an older brother seriously. His younger brother, Andre, watches and mimics his every move—so Felipe knows he's setting a standard.

To Felipe, life is about action—not waiting for things to happen, but making them happen.

One crisp fall morning, as they walk through the crowded streets toward the community center, Felipe shares a new plan. The local park has become rundown—trash scattered, equipment rusting, benches broken. It bothers him.

"Let's clean this up," he says.

Andre hesitates but nods, and together, they commit. What starts as a small cleanup turns into something bigger. Their efforts spark a wave of pride through the neighborhood. Parents pitch in. Teens stop by to help. The park starts looking like a place kids actually want to be.

Andre beams, knowing it all started with Felipe. He watches his brother differently now—not just with admiration, but with intention. He starts showing up in new ways, inspired to lead too.

Word spreads about what the two brothers did. But Felipe stays grounded. He reminds Andre, "Leadership isn't about being loud or having a title. It's about seeing what needs to be done—and doing it."

THE EMOTIONAL ROLLERCOASTER

THE EMOTIONAL ROLLERCOASTER

That moment becomes a turning point for Andre. He sees that being proactive isn't just about solving problems—it's about becoming the kind of person who makes things better, wherever you go.

Their park project doesn't just fix a space. It rewrites the narrative for their neighborhood, showing that small actions can spark big changes—especially when led by someone willing to go first.

Meanwhile, 22-year-old Isaac—a senior baseball player facing the loss of his starting position—wrestles with a very different kind of leadership: learning how to lead from behind.

SIQ Tip: Life is not about expecting, hoping and wishing. It's about doing, being and becoming.

ATTITUDE ADJUSTMENT

Isaac, a 22-year-old college senior and once standout baseball player, is stuck in a brutal slump. After losing his starting spot on the team, his confidence nosedives. Mentally and academically, he spirals. He blames his coaches for favoritism, his professors for being unfair. Everything feels stacked against him.

One evening, overwhelmed and frustrated, Isaac calls his younger sister to vent. She listens quietly, then offers something unexpected: "Maybe it's not them, Isaac. How might adjusting your attitude change what your days feel like? One of the best things about attitude is it's free—and you get to choose it every day."

68

That hits a nerve. The next week, Isaac gives her advice a shot. He approaches his coach—not with excuses, but with an apology and a request: "Can you give me feedback on my defensive game?" In class, he shifts too—asking his professors how he can actually improve, then following through.

Slowly, the tide starts turning. Not through luck, but through his actions.

His coaches start coaching him again—really coaching. His grades climb. But more than that, Isaac starts to feel something he hasn't felt in months: control. Not over everything—but over how he shows up.

He stops blaming. Starts owning. That shift—simple but powerful—changes everything. Isaac realizes he might not control every outcome, but he does control his effort, his energy, and his attitude. And that changes the way the world responds to him.

As Isaac finds strength in ownership, 19-year-old Andrew, a college freshman, sits in a psychology lecture, wondering something similar—can understanding emotions help him beat his brutal test anxiety?

SIQ Tip: Performance follows attitude.

ANXIETY ANSWERS
Andrew, a 19-year-old college freshman, sits nervously in the back of his Psychology 101 class, hands clenched under the desk. His mind races with anxiety before every exam. But today's lecture on emotional intelligence sparks something—hope.

THE EMOTIONAL ROLLERCOASTER

The professor explains how self-awareness and emotional regulation can reshape how we handle pressure. Andrew leans in. For the first time, he wonders: what if anxiety isn't something to suffer through, but something he can manage?

That day, he commits to a new approach. He starts applying just two techniques from class: naming his emotions and understanding what triggers them. He soon adds a short daily meditation to his morning routine and practices positive self-talk to challenge the spiral of negative thoughts.

Over the next few months, his seven minutes a day turns into new habits, leading to new outcomes. And with it, a different version of Andrew starts showing up. Not frozen by panic—but calm. Focused. Ready.

When midterms hit, Andrew doesn't collapse under pressure. He welcomes it. He doesn't just pass—he crushes it.

That moment rewires something deeper. Andrew realizes emotional intelligence isn't just about exams. It's life armor. A skillset for every challenge.

And as Andrew grows more confident, we meet Sky, a 15-year-old freshman facing a very different kind of emotional storm during a bitter Pennsylvania November. A breakup. A string of disappointments. And a battle she's losing against her own overreactions.

SIQ Tip: Emotional intelligence can be worked on but not measured. And remember, not everything that counts can be counted.

TURMOIL TURNAROUND

In the middle of a frigid November in Pennsylvania, 15-year-old Sky is going through it. A high school freshman, she's reeling from a string of brutal personal setbacks, including a breakup that leaves her emotionally wrecked. Each hit seems heavier than the last, and Sky's reactions grow more intense. The frustration, the mood swings—it all feels nonstop.

One evening, after an especially bad day, Sky breaks down in front of her mom—her confidante, her anchor. Her mom listens quietly, then gently asks, "Honey, how do you feel your responses to challenging situations shape your experiences?"

Sky scoffs at it at first but the question sticks. That night, she starts looking for answers. She dives into mindfulness, starts journaling her emotions, and sets small daily goals—just enough to feel like progress on even the hardest days.

Slowly, her emotional surges don't control her the way they used to. The energy that once exploded in anger or sadness now channels into action—cleaning her room, finishing a project, texting a friend instead of bottling things up.

People around her notice. She handles drama with surprising calm. Her bounce-back time after setbacks shortens. She's still facing the same chaos as before, but somehow, she's different—happier, more grounded, more in control.

Sky goes from being overwhelmed by emotion to owning it. Her ability to turn emotional spirals into steady progress catches attention. It even inspires others—including 18-year-old Chase, a senior quietly drowning in distractions and struggling to stay focused as graduation looms.

THE EMOTIONAL ROLLERCOASTER

SIQ Tip: When I encounter setbacks and failures, I must avoid overreacting to them.

SENIOR SURGE

In the bustling corridors of his high school, 18-year-old Chase feels the relentless pull of senioritis tugging at his concentration. As the final semester of his senior year unwinds, the excitement of graduation mixes with a daunting lack of motivation. He watches classmates succumb to the lethargy that seems almost ritualistic, but deep down, he wants to finish strong.

One chilly evening, feeling lost, Chase FaceTimes his older brother Alex, a college sophomore. After listening, Alex asks, "Chase, do you believe persistence can be developed like a muscle?" Chase says, "Sure." Alex follows up, "So what small, daily habits could you put in place to build that persistence?"

The next day, Chase starts small. He breaks down assignments into manageable tasks. Each completed step builds momentum. The infamous feeling of senioritis begins to lift.

By the time he delivers his valedictorian speech, he reflects on how choosing discipline over chance changed not just his grades—but how he approaches challenges.

Now we turn to Micah, a 21-year-old college junior and tennis player, who is struggling with his own motivation crisis. After a series of underwhelming performances on the court, Micah's confidence is completely plummeting.

SIQ Tip: Persistence can only be practiced if I follow through and consistently perform the things I say I will.

COURT CONFIDENCE

Micah grips his racket tighter as another serve sails into the net. His teammates exchange worried glances—this isn't the same player who dominates freshman year. The crushing pressure of junior year has turned tennis from his sanctuary into a brutal battlefield of self-doubt.

That evening, Micah sits alone in his dorm, scrolling through old match videos. A few clips in, he notices something obvious but devastating: in his best matches, his body language oozes confidence—the way he walks, stands, and celebrates. But in recent games, his shoulders slump before he even steps onto the court. That small shift affects everything. His mental state isn't just influencing his performance—it's reshaping it.

Micah decides to try something different with his mindset. Each morning, he spends just five minutes visualizing: successful serves, decisive footwork, and confident returns. He builds a pre-match ritual—three deep breaths, a shoulder roll, and a reminder: "I belong here because..." followed by four reasons.

He also adds a new habit: tracking his thoughts during practice, catching negative self-talk before it poisons his play.

The change isn't instant, but it's steady. Within two weeks, his serve speed climbs over 10 mph and stays there. His backhand, once tentative, becomes sharp and aggressive. By the time the conference championship arrives, Micah feels that familiar surge of belief. His body follows his mind's lead, and he plays with the fluidity he thought he'd lost.

When Micah lifts the championship trophy for the first time, a deeper truth settles in: athletic growth isn't just about physical reps—your mental game sculpts every part of performance. Confidence isn't something you wait for. It's built, one intentional thought at a time.

His mindset becomes his secret weapon, proving that sometimes the strongest muscle you can train is the one between your ears.

Meanwhile, 400 miles north in muggy Michigan, 24-year-old Reagan presses her paint-stained fingers against the dew-covered window of her studio apartment. The warm June morning matches her creative drought perfectly. Once a promising dancer whose career ended with a devastating injury, she's thrown herself into painting, but something pivotal is missing.

SIQ Tip: Development is very sensitive and will affect my overall mental state including: performance, participation, confidence and motivation.

MINDFUL MOVES
Reagan stares at her reflection in the damp window, seeing not just her face but the ghost of who she used to be. The dancer who once commands stages with raw emotion now struggles to infuse even a whisper of feeling into her paintings.

Then it happens—unexpectedly, in a moment of pure frustration. Scraping paint off her palette in anger, she accidentally smears crimson across the canvas. It should ruin the piece. Instead, the chaotic streak captures something her careful brushstrokes never can—pure, unfiltered emotion.

She begins an experiment that changes everything. Before each painting session, she sits quietly and names exactly what she's feeling: grief for her lost dance career, fear of mediocrity, excitement about new possibilities. She discovers her body holds emotional memories differently than her mind. When painting landscapes, she recalls the physical sensation of landing a perfect grand jeté—the way her chest opens with triumph, how her fingertips spark with electricity.

The shift is instant and undeniable. Her paintings pulse with real emotion—viewers don't just see them; they feel them. A simple portrait of an elderly man now captures not only his weathered features but the weight of decades behind his eyes. Gallery visitors stop longer, drawn to something they can't quite name but deeply feel.

Standing before her latest masterpiece—a swirling abstract that somehow captures the bittersweet beauty of dreams deferred—Reagan realizes emotions aren't just something to understand. They're a language of the heart, translated through art to help others feel less alone.

A few states south, in the sprawling suburbs of Las Vegas, 16-year-old Damian sits in his car after school, engine off, unable to face going inside. Another day of pretending everything is fine while anxiety gnaws at his stomach. His friends see the funny, confident kid; his parents see good grades and extracurricular success. But Damian feels like he's drowning in expectations.

THE EMOTIONAL ROLLERCOASTER

SIQ Tip: Emotional intelligence is just as important as physical gifts in life.

SOPHOMORE STRESS

Damian sits in his car, gripping the steering wheel as waves of anxiety crash over him. The "perfect" teenager everyone sees—honor roll student, varsity soccer player, class treasurer—feels like a prison he's built around his true self. Every achievement only raises the bar higher, and the fear of disappointing anyone keeps him awake most nights, staring at the ceiling while his mind races through tomorrow's endless to-do list.

The breaking point comes during a panic attack in AP Chemistry. While his classmates focus intently on molecular structures, Damian's chest tightens like a vise, his vision blurs at the edges, and he bolts from the room without explanation. Sitting alone in the bathroom, hunched over on the cold tile floor, he realizes he can't keep pretending anymore—the mask of perfection is suffocating him.

That evening, Damian makes a hard decision: he will start paying attention to his emotions instead of stuffing them down like he's been trained to do his entire life. He begins setting phone alarms three times a day with a simple but revolutionary question: "How am I really feeling right now?" At first, the answers are frustratingly vague—"stressed," "tired," "fine"—surface-level responses that reveal nothing. But gradually, he discovers a complex emotional landscape he's been systematically ignoring for years.

With some help from AI and online resources, Damian learns to distinguish between different types of anxiety: the sharp, cutting edge of academic pressure feels completely different from the hollow, persistent ache of social expectations. He starts naming his emotions out loud to his reflection each morning, and something remarkable happens—simply acknowledging his feelings begins to defuse their overwhelming power over him.

Damian's real moment of discovery comes when he stops trying to "fix" his emotions and starts treating them as valuable information about his inner world. His anxiety often signals he's overcommitted; his irritability usually means he desperately needs alone time to recharge. Instead of fighting these feelings like enemies, he begins acknowledging them as allies.

By spring semester, Damian still feels the intense pressures of high school, but he's developed emotional fluency—the ability to read his internal compass and make choices that align with his authentic self rather than everyone else's relentless expectations.

Meanwhile, in the thin mountain air of Boulder, Colorado, 16-year-old Natalia slams her bedroom door so hard the picture frames rattle violently on the walls. Another explosive fight with her mom, another bridge burned with her best friend, another reputation-destroying outburst in the school hallway. Her hot temper has become her defining trait, and she's tired of the wreckage it leaves behind.

SIQ Tip: How do I prioritize my mental and emotional well-being? What's one habit I can develop to support this?

FIELDED FEELINGS

Natalia's fist stops inches from her bedroom wall as she catches her reflection in the mirror—red-faced, tears streaming, looking exactly like the out-of-control kid everyone expects her to be. This has to stop.

The catalyst comes from an unlikely source: her 8-year-old cousin Emma, who witnesses Natalia's latest meltdown at a family dinner. "Why do you get so scary-angry?" Emma asks innocently, her wide eyes filled with genuine curiosity rather than judgment. The question hits harder than any lecture from parents or teachers ever has, cutting straight through Natalia's defenses to the core of who she's become.

Natalia begins paying more attention to her anger, approaching it like a science experiment rather than a character flaw to hide. She discovers her rage has distinct warning signs: a tightness in her jaw that spreads like a wire being pulled, heat rising steadily in her chest, her hands clenching into fists without her conscious awareness. Most importantly, she realizes her anger is often masking deeper, more vulnerable emotions—feeling hurt when friends exclude her from plans, fear when she feels misunderstood or judged, disappointment when she lets herself down.

She develops what she calls her "fire pause"—the crucial moment she feels anger building, she takes three deep breaths and asks herself with genuine curiosity: "What am I really feeling underneath this?" The technique doesn't eliminate her natural intensity, but it gives her choices she never knew she had. Instead of exploding at her best friend for canceling plans, she recognizes her hurt and communicates it directly, opening space for real connection.

Meaningful change isn't about suppressing her fire—it's about directing it toward something constructive. Natalia channels her passion into advocacy, becoming the fearless voice for kids who feel misunderstood and overlooked. Her intensity, once destructive and isolating, becomes her superpower for fighting injustice and standing up for others.

Standing before the school board months later, passionately defending a bullied classmate with articulate fury, Natalia realizes she hasn't lost her fire—she's learned to wield it with surgical precision.

Meanwhile, across the country in Nashville, Tennessee, 22-year-old Ashton sits behind his drum kit in his cramped apartment, sticks idle in his hands. Six months ago, choosing music over a "stable" career path felt like destiny calling his name. Now, scrolling through LinkedIn and watching former classmates land corporate jobs with steady paychecks and clear advancement paths, doubt creeps in like morning fog.

SIQ Tip: Control my emotions, or my emotions will control me. Don't make permanent decisions based on temporary emotions.

SOUND DECISION
Ashton stares at his phone screen, watching another college friend post about their promotion, their shiny new car, their carefully curated "adulting" milestones. Meanwhile, his dinner consists of ramen noodles and the crushing weight of second-guessing every life choice he's made in the past year.

The doubt hits hardest at 3AM when he can't sleep, his mind relentlessly calculating how much money he could have made in a corporate job instead of grinding in smoky dive bars for twenty bucks and free beer. His parents' disappointed sighs echo in his memory every time he misses another family dinner because of a gig, their unspoken "we told you so" hanging heavy in the air.

The breaking point comes during a particularly brutal practice session. His bandmates are discussing their backup plans—law school, teaching, marketing jobs—while Ashton realizes with growing panic that he's burned those bridges completely. The fear feels overwhelming: *What if I'm just delusional? What if I'm wasting my twenties chasing a fantasy that everyone else can see is hopeless?*

But then he notices something during their next performance. Mid-song, watching a couple slow dance to their music, seeing complete strangers sing along to lyrics he wrote alone in his bedroom at 2AM, Ashton feels it—the pure, electric connection that made him choose this uncertain path. This isn't just about personal success or proving people wrong; it's about creating moments that genuinely matter to people who need them.

He starts reframing FOMO as information rather than torture. His friends' achievements aren't evidence of his failure; they're simply different paths leading to different destinations that suit different souls. More importantly, he realizes that meaningful work often looks like failure from the outside while it's being painstakingly built.

Ashton learns to measure success differently—not by Instagram posts or salary figures, but by artistic growth, sustained passion, and the profound impact his music has on people who desperately need it. The FOMO never completely disappears, but it no longer has the power to derail his dreams or make him abandon what feels most authentic.

THE EMOTIONAL ROLLERCOASTER

Meanwhile, in a humid Maryland pool, 17-year-old Ivy treads water during a timeout, her mind already replaying the three shots she's missed in agonizing detail. As the only exchange student on the water polo team, every mistake feels magnified under a microscope, every small victory diminished by her own brutal, unforgiving self-criticism.

SIQ Tip: Reframing comparison as information rather than self-torture, allowing me to stay committed to my authentic path despite external pressures is key.

DEEP DIVE

Ivy floats in the Maryland pool during halftime, her teammates' encouraging shouts muffled underwater as her internal critic screams louder than ever. Three missed shots, two defensive lapses—her mind keeps a brutal scorecard that no coach would ever use. Being the only exchange student feels like swimming with weights; every mistake seems to confirm she doesn't belong here.

Her change in perspective starts with an accidental eavesdrop. Ivy overhears her teammate Sarah beating herself up after a bad practice: "I'm so stupid, I suck at this." Hearing those harsh words from someone else makes Ivy realize how toxic her own self-talk has become. She'd never speak to a friend the way she speaks to herself—the cruelty is shocking when she recognizes it.

Ivy tries something that changes her course. Instead of her usual post-mistake ritual of self-destruction, she starts asking: "What would I say to my little sister if she made this mistake?" The answers are always kinder, more constructive, more focused on learning than punishment. The contrast is startling—she has endless compassion for others but reserves only criticism for herself.

She pays attention to and recognizes her harsh internal voice in the act and consciously replaces it with the tone she'd use with a struggling teammate. When she misses a shot, instead of "You're worthless," it becomes "Next play, Ivy. You've got this." The shift feels awkward at first, like speaking a foreign language.

She puts her small tweak to the ultimate test during the regional championships. Down by two with seconds left, Ivy has a clear shot. Her old voice whispers familiar doubts about not belonging here, but her new voice says firmly, "This is why you trained. Show them what commitment looks like."

She scores! But more importantly, she celebrates without immediately thinking about what she could have done better. Ivy has learned to be her own teammate, not her own enemy—the most important relationship shift of her athletic career.

Meanwhile, at the University of Wisconsin, 20-year-old competitive diver Felicia stands at the edge of the ten-meter platform, her mind as sharp and disciplined as her form. Known for her unshakeable mental toughness and positive self-talk, she's earned her spot at the upcoming US Olympic Trials through her consistency and mental fortitude.

SIQ Tip: Be mindful to replace harsh self-criticism with supportive self-coaching, treating myself with the same compassion I'd show a friend.

THE EMOTIONAL ROLLERCOASTER

PLATFORM PRESSURES

Felicia stands on the ten-meter platform at the Olympic Trials, her usual pre-dive mantra running through her mind: "Strong body, stronger mind. You've earned this moment." For three years, this mental formula has been bulletproof. But today, with cameras rolling and her parents in the stands, something feels different.

The first dive goes perfectly—her signature inward two-and-a-half somersault that has dominated college competitions. But as she climbs for her second dive, doubt creeps in like water through a crack. *What if I choke? What if my mental toughness leaves me when I need it most?*

The second dive wobbles slightly on entry. Not enough to eliminate her, but enough to shatter her usual unshakeable composure. Felicia feels her carefully constructed mental fortress beginning to crumble. Her positive self-talk, once automatic, now feels forced and hollow.

That's when Felicia realizes something crucial: true mental toughness isn't about never feeling doubt—it's about performing while feeling it. She stops trying to eliminate the pressure and starts acknowledging it. "Yes, I'm nervous. Yes, this matters. And yes, I belong here."

She begins treating her nerves as fuel rather than obstacles. The third dive, her most challenging, requires her to channel that nervous energy into explosive power. Instead of fighting the butterflies, she lets them lift her higher. Her entry is flawless—the kind of dive that makes the pool go silent.

Standing on the platform for her final dive, Felicia realizes her mental armor hasn't failed her—it has evolved. She's learned that authentic confidence includes doubt, fear, and pressure. Mental toughness isn't about being invincible; it's about being real and performing through it.

Her final dive secures her spot on the Olympic team, but more importantly, it teaches her that vulnerability and strength can coexist.

Then there's Destiny. A 17-year-old junior volleyball player with dreams of playing in college. However, off the court, Destiny is navigating the turbulent emotions of a recent breakup with her boyfriend of three years and the paralyzing fear of speaking up. The breakup has left her feeling destroyed and unsure about her future in volleyball.

SIQ Tip: The mind leads and the body follows.

RALLY RESILIENCE

Destiny sits in the back row of the team meeting, her usual spot as starting setter now feeling foreign. Since Chris broke up with her three weeks ago—via text, after three years together—everything feels wrong. The worst part isn't just losing him; it's losing her voice entirely.

Before the breakup, Destiny was the team's vocal leader, calling plays with confidence, rallying teammates during tough matches. Now she barely whispers during drills, terrified that speaking up will somehow expose how broken she feels inside. Her college recruitment dreams feel as shattered as her heart does.

The tipping point comes during a crucial match against their biggest rivals. Destiny watches a perfect setup opportunity slip away because she can't bring herself to call for the ball.

Her silence costs them the point, possibly the match, maybe her future.

That night, staring at old photos with Chris on her phone, Destiny realizes something devastating: she's built her identity around being half of a couple. When he left, he took her confidence with him. But volleyball was hers long before he was—she needs to remember that truth.

Destiny starts small—calling a few plays in practice, then a few more. She begins journaling before bed, rediscovering pieces of herself that exist independently of any relationship. Most importantly, she learns to distinguish between her voice as Chris's girlfriend and her voice as Destiny the athlete, the leader, the person who exists fully on her own.

She has more mental clarity and confidence during her next match. Down two sets, Destiny feels the familiar urge to shrink away and disappear. Instead, she stands up and addresses her team with renewed fire: "We've got this. Trust me, trust each other, and let's chip away at this thing. Focus on our next—that's it! Our next play, our next moment, our next point. Let's go!"

They win in five sets. But more importantly, Destiny has found something Chris's departure couldn't take away—her authentic voice, stronger for having been tested by heartbreak and rebuilt from within.

Now we shift to Kendall, whose story picks up on a cold late May night in the Midwest. At 18, Kendall is struggling with a hard home life that makes her other challenges seem trivial. Her dad's alcoholism and violent behavior toward her mom casts a long shadow over her mental and emotional well-being. His constant yelling makes concentrating on homework feel impossible for as long as she can remember.

SIQ Tip: Rebuilding my authentic self-expression after trauma by separating my core identity from external relationships or circumstances is one of the most important skills I can learn.

SAFE SPACE

Kendall presses her back against her bedroom door, trying to muffle the sound of her father's drunken rage echoing through their thin-walled house. At 18, she's become an expert at reading the warning signs—the heavy footsteps, the slurred accusations, the inevitable crash of something breaking. Tonight feels worse than usual.

Her Pre-Calc homework lies scattered across her desk, equations blurring through tears she refuses to let fall. How can she solve any equations when her entire world feels like an unsolvable problem? Her grades are tanking, her teacher keeps asking if everything is okay at home, and Kendall feels like she's drowning in chaos she can't control.

An unexpected source helps Kendall think of things a little differently: her school counselor's simple question during a mandatory check-in. "Kendall, what's one thing that feels completely yours, that no one else can touch?" The answer surprises her: the twenty minutes she spends each morning before anyone else wakes up, sitting by her window with her small breakfast, watching the sunrise paint the sky in soft colors.

Kendall begins building what she calls her "inner fortress"— small rituals and mental spaces that belong only to her. She starts each day with breathing exercises as part of her sacred morning routine. When chaos erupts downstairs, she retreats to mental visualization of a peaceful space her grandmother described from her childhood in Mexico.

Most importantly, Kendall learns to separate her worth from her circumstances. Her father's illness isn't her fault or her failure. Her mother's pain isn't her responsibility to fix. Her grades can recover, but only if she protects her mental health first.

Things don't change radically overnight, but the changes are noticeable. Kendall still lives in the same house, hears the same fights, but she's created an inner foundation that no external storm can destroy. She's learned to be her own sanctuary.

Meanwhile, in a trendy downtown apartment, 22-year-old Aidan stares at his reflection in his phone camera, adjusting the filter for the third time. Fresh out of college and drowning in a world where everyone seems effortlessly perfect, he can't scroll through social media without feeling like a rough draft among published masterpieces.

SIQ Tip: Being able to overcome some of my biggest fears and unknowns is possible. I have to remind myself, where I'm going is more important than where I am.

FILTER FREE
Aidan stares at his reflection in his phone camera, adjusting the filter for the fourth time. The Valencia filter makes his skin glow, but still can't hide what he sees as fundamental flaws. Fresh out of college, he'd expected to feel confident

and ready for the world. Instead, every mirror feels like evidence of his inadequacy.

The spiral started innocently enough—just using filters "for fun." But somewhere between the perfect selfies and endless scrolling through influencers with impossible bodies, Aidan loses sight of his real face. Without a filter, he looks alien to himself. Too pale, too many freckles, not the right kind of attractive that gets thousands of likes.

His low point comes during a job interview conducted over video call. Sitting in front of his laptop, unable to use filters, Aidan feels exposed and hideous. He can barely make eye contact with the camera, convinced the interviewer is judging his appearance instead of his qualifications. He doesn't get the job.

That night, crying in his bathroom, Aidan makes a rash decision: he deletes all his photo editing apps. The first week is brutal—seeing his unfiltered face feels like meeting a stranger. But slowly, something shifts. He starts noticing details filters had erased: the constellation of freckles his grandmother called "angel kisses," the way his eyes crinkle when he genuinely smiles.

Aidan begins practicing what he calls "reality training"— taking one unfiltered photo each day, not to post, just to get comfortable with his actual appearance. He unfollows accounts that make him feel inadequate and starts following photographers who celebrate natural beauty and diversity.

The change is gradual and important. Standing in front of his mirror six months later, filter-free, Aidan sees himself clearly for the first time in years. Not perfect, not Instagram-ready, but authentically human—and that feels revolutionary.

THE EMOTIONAL ROLLERCOASTER

Across town, 21-year-old Quinn sits in her apartment surrounded by the blue glow of multiple screens—phone, laptop, gaming console all pinging with notifications from her 30,000 online "friends." Yet despite all this connectivity, she's never felt more profoundly alone. *How can someone be so connected, yet feel so invisible at the same time?*

SIQ Tip: It's so important to develop an authentic self-image by disconnecting my self-worth from digital perfection and reconnecting with unfiltered reality.

SCREEN DEEP

Quinn scrolls through her phone at 2AM, notifications from hundreds of "friends" lighting up her screen. Discord, Instagram, Snapchat—constant digital noise that somehow makes the silence in her apartment feel deafening. Despite being part of a generation more "connected" than any prior generation in human history, Quinn still feels invisible.

This feeling really hits home on her 21st birthday. Her social media explodes with generic "Happy Birthday!" messages from people she barely knows, but when she looks around her empty apartment ordering DoorDash alone, Quinn realizes something devastating: she doesn't have a single person she can actually call to hang out.

She's confused online engagement with real friendship. All these digital relationships feel like eating cotton candy—sweet in the moment but leaving her hollow and hungry for something substantial. Group video calls with college friends just make it worse; everyone talks over each other, jokes get lost in lag, and Quinn feels like a spectator watching life happen to everyone else.

THE EMOTIONAL ROLLERCOASTER

Desperate for something to change, Quinn joins a local photography meetup. Standing awkwardly with her camera, she almost leaves three times. But then another girl, equally nervous, asks about her lens. They spend two hours walking downtown, actually talking—not typing, not posting, just being present with each other, sharing space with another human being.

That conversation leads to coffee, then to genuine friendship. It leads to Quinn understanding the profound difference between being connected and being seen. Online, she's just a profile picture and witty comments. In person, she's a whole person with quirks, hesitations, and genuine thoughts that can't fit in a text bubble.

Six months later, Quinn still uses social media, but it no longer defines her social life. She's learned that real connection requires vulnerability, presence, and the messy, imperfect beauty of face-to-face humanity that can't be filtered or edited.

Meanwhile, in another part of the country, 18-year-old Chloe sits in her dorm room staring at lines of code that could revolutionize machine learning. Her AI model is performing beyond anything her professors have seen from an undergraduate, yet she can't shake the feeling that she's a fraud about to be exposed.

SIQ Tip: Distinguishing between digital connectivity and authentic human connection is an important distinction for me to understand. Prioritizing quality relationships over quantity of online interactions is a key factor to live a healthy life.

IMPOSTER SYNDROME

The notification pops up on Chloe's screen: "Your paper has been accepted for the International AI Conference." At 18, she's just become the youngest person ever invited to present at the world's most prestigious artificial intelligence summit. But instead of celebrating, Chloe feels nauseated.

They're going to realize I don't belong here, her inner critic whispers insistently. *I just got lucky with this algorithm. Real computer scientists will see right through me.*

For months, Chloe has been paralyzed by imposter syndrome. Despite her neural network achieving 97% accuracy—a breakthrough that could transform healthcare diagnostics— she convinces herself it's a fluke. She's almost deleted the entire project three times, certain it's garbage that will embarrass her in front of the academic community.

Chloe experiences a turning point during a late-night coding session when her roommate finds her crying over her laptop. "Chloe," she says gently, "what would you tell a friend who created something this incredible?" The question makes Chloe actually pause for a moment. She'd never speak to a friend the way she speaks to herself—the cruelty is shocking when she recognizes it.

Chloe begins documenting and being more aware of her journey. Instead of focusing on what she doesn't know, she starts listing what she's taught herself: advanced calculus at 16, machine learning architectures, three programming languages. She realizes expertise isn't about knowing everything—it's about being brave enough to explore the unknown and persist through confusion.

THE EMOTIONAL ROLLERCOASTER

Standing before 2,000 of the world's top AI researchers, Chloe feels her hands shake as she clicks to her first slide. But then she remembers something: they aren't there to judge her worthiness—they're there because her work could save lives.

Her presentation is flawless. But more importantly, Chloe finally understands that brilliance isn't about feeling confident—it's about doing extraordinary work despite feeling scared. Imposter syndrome hasn't disappeared, but it no longer has the power to silence her potential or stop her from sharing her gifts with the world.

SIQ Tip: Treat myself with the same compassion I'd show a friend.

PART 3

CHASING HAPPINESS

CHASING HAPPINESS

What if the thing that's supposed to make you happy is actually destroying your mental health?

Meet Mason—17, chronically online, and stuck in the perfectionism trap that's killing so many peoples' joy, including his own. He's got a drawer full of half-finished projects because nothing feels "good enough" to share. Sound familiar?

But here's the unlikely reason he finds to change; or maybe it found him? One random TikTok notification.

What follows isn't the perfect success story. It's the messy, real journey of learning to choose your battles—from football drama to family expectations, from social media pressure to actual substance use. Mason discovers that chasing happiness means making seemingly impossible choices between dreams and family, success and mental health, being yourself and fitting in. And one of the hardest lessons? Sometimes the people you love most, make you feel the most invisible.

Through anxiety, heartbreak, college struggles, and finding his tribe, Mason learns that happiness isn't a destination you reach—it's a skill you build, one imperfect day at a time. By looking for and recognizing more things in life, not waiting for the few fleeting moments others tell you about.

I again conclude many of the entries in Part 3 with a SIQ Tip (simple, immediate, quick) to challenge you to live an even better life, sooner.

CHASING HAPPINESS

HAPPINESS HUSTLE

I stare at my desk drawer—a graveyard of half-finished projects. Unfinished beats on my laptop. A skateboard design I've sketched but never built. Code for an app that would revolutionize my school, abandoned after the first bug.

My phone buzzes. A random TikTok notification from an account I've never followed: *"Some is better than none. Done is better than perfect."*

For some reason, the words hit different today. I look at my latest victim—a short film project due tomorrow that I've restarted six times because the lighting isn't cinematic enough.

"Screw it," I mutter, grabbing my phone. I film the entire thing in one take, using natural lighting from my bedroom window. No fancy transitions. No perfect angles. Just... done.

When I post it to my story, the responses flood in. "This is fire!" "Bro, the raw style hits hard."

The rush is intoxicating. I spend the next three days finishing a few other projects I've abandoned. I upload my beats to SoundCloud—they aren't Grammy-worthy, but kids at school are already asking to use them. I code my app's basic version and watch classmates download it within hours.

For the first time in months, I feel... accomplished. Like I'm actually living instead of just planning to live.

The success is addictive. Each completed project builds momentum for the next. My confidence soars as my "done" pile grows and my "perfect someday" pile shrinks to almost nothing.

CHASING HAPPINESS

But Friday afternoon changes everything.

Coach Sander pulls me aside after football practice. "College scouts are coming next month, Mason. You've got real potential." The words should thrill me, but I feel my stomach drop.

As I walk to the parking lot, cleats echoing on the concrete, I spot the track team finishing their workout. The way they move—fluid, powerful, free—sparks something inside me I've never felt watching football film.

I've played football since I was seven. It's all anyone knows me for. But what if I'm meant for something else entirely?

What happens when the thing you're best at isn't the thing that makes you feel most alive?

SIQ Tip: Some is better than none; done is better than perfect.

CHORD CHOICES

I stand in Guitar Center, staring at a beat-up acoustic that costs more than saving my monthly allowance for nearly a year. Football two-a-days start next week, but something about the instrument calls to me louder than any coach's whistle ever has.

"Done is better than perfect," I whisper, remembering my new mantra. I buy it.

The first week is brutal. My fingertips bleed from the steel strings, and every chord sounds like nails on a chalkboard.

CHASING HAPPINESS

But when I finally nail my first clean G major, the rush hits different than any touchdown celebration.

I start sneaking guitar practice between football workouts, posting progress videos to my close friends story. My followers eat it up—comments like "didn't know you had this in you" and "this is actually fire" keep me motivated through the learning curve.

Three months in, everything changes. A local indie band called Midnight Static finds my videos through a mutual friend's repost. Their lead guitarist is graduating, and they need someone with my raw energy and willingness to learn.

"We've got gigs lined up through spring," their drummer Jake explains over FaceTime. "Nothing huge, but some decent venues. You in?"

My heart races. This is it—my chance to be known for something other than how many yards I can rush for.

But then reality hits. Band practice is Saturdays. Gigs are weekend nights. My little sister Emma's soccer games are Saturdays. My mom's birthday dinner is next Saturday. My grandpa's Sunday family dinners have been tradition since… forever.

I stare at my phone, caught between two group chats—one with my bandmates planning their next rehearsal, another with my family discussing weekend plans.

For the first time since discovering my "done is better than perfect" philosophy, I feel paralyzed again. Choosing my music means disappointing people who've supported me long before I ever picked up a guitar. But choosing family means potentially missing my shot at something that makes me feel truly alive.

Is happiness worth becoming the person who breaks promises to the people who matter most?

SIQ Tip: What I've always done does not define me. Starting something new and adding to who I am and what I do is an important ingredient to build my self-belief.

FAMILIES & DREAMS
Earlier today I'm standing in my room holding my guitar, listening to my family laugh downstairs at game night. They're probably wondering where I am. Mom makes her famous nachos. Emma's probably crushing Dad at Monopoly right now.

But Midnight Static is *this close* to landing the Brew & Bean gig. Jake texts saying we could nail the setlist today if everyone shows up focused.

My hands are literally shaking. When did choosing between family and following your passion become this hard?

Just got home from practice. We were ON FIRE tonight. I hit every single note on "Electric Nights," and even wrote a bridge that made Jake's jaw drop. The energy was insane— like we're actually becoming a real band.

But the house is dead quiet now. Game night's over. Emma's door is closed. I can hear her watching TikToks alone.

CHASING HAPPINESS

The leftover nachos are still on the counter, cold and sad-looking. There's a sticky note from Mom: "Saved you some! Hope practice went well. 🩶"

Why does doing what makes me happy feel so selfish?

Mr. Peterson hands back our history projects. C-. A literal C- stares up at me like a disappointment trophy.

I spent two weeks on this thing, but I know I was distracted. Half my research time got eaten up by guitar practice. My mind kept drifting to chord progressions during study sessions.

This is the third mediocre grade in a row. Mom's going to notice soon—she checks my grades religiously on the parent portal. The worst part though? I'm not even sure I care anymore. Like, when am I ever going to need to know about the Industrial Revolution when I'm playing sold-out shows?

But what if the music thing doesn't work out? What if I'm just some kid with a guitar and a dream, letting everything else fall apart?

Is chasing happiness supposed to make everything else in your life feel like it's crumbling?

SIQ Tip: When to be selfish vs selfless. There's time to do both.

STUDY BREAKTHROUGH

Last week, I get my third C- this month. I'm literally staring at the chemistry test like it's written in a foreign language. My confidence… gone.

CHASING HAPPINESS

I keep wondering—why can I nail a complicated guitar solo but bomb a simple test about molecules? It doesn't make sense.

And I couldn't sleep last night. My brain keeps replaying every wrong answer, every confused moment in class. But then something weird hits me.

Remember when Midnight Static learned "Neon Dreams"? We didn't just run through it once and expect perfection. Jake made us practice each section separately. We built it piece by piece until the whole song flowed.

School isn't that different from music. I've just been treating it like it is.

So, I decide to try something. I treat my history essay like learning a new song. Break it into verses—research, outline, intro, body, conclusion. Spend real time on each part instead of cramming everything the night before.

When I turn it in, I actually feel... prepared. Like I know what I'm doing for once.

Then today happens. Ms. Rodriguez hands back my essay. A- ... AN ACTUAL A-!

I try not to smile like an idiot in class, but I feel like I just nailed a solo in front of a packed venue. My confidence is creeping back.

But then dinner gets weird. Matt slams his homework shut and starts getting frustrated. "I can't remember any of these stupid state capitals," he mutters, looking defeated.

CHASING HAPPINESS

Watching him struggle is hard for me. He looks exactly like me a few weeks ago—defeated, frustrated, ready to give up.

I pull out my phone and show him this AI app I've been using for guitar practice. "What if we make it fun? Like a game?"

We use AI to create silly songs about each state capital. "Denver, Denver, Colorado's the place to be!" Matt is cracking up, but more importantly, he's learning.

When he finally gets them all right, his smile is bigger than mine was this morning. And I think, if I can find my own path to success, maybe I can help others find theirs too. But is that my responsibility, or should I focus on keeping my own life together first?

SIQ Tip: I build confidence through preparation and reps. Keep the promises I tell myself.

LIFTING UP

I get another chemistry test back today. An A! Another A! I'm still staring at it in disbelief. After weeks of feeling like I'm bombing everything, I finally crack the code—preparation isn't cramming the night before. It's like learning guitar. Small steps, repetition, focus. The same method actually works for something else.

The rush of seeing that grade is incredible, but something even better happens this past weekend.

Emma is sitting at the kitchen table, staring at her math homework like it personally offends her. "I hate fractions," she mumbles, not even touching the sandwich Mom made for her.

CHASING HAPPINESS

I know that exact feeling. The frustration, the defeat, the wanting to give up before you even try.

"Math's like music," I tell her. "There's a rhythm to it. Want me to show you?"

She rolls her eyes but lets me sit next to her. We work through the problems like beats in a song—steady, one after another, building the pattern. When she finally gets that first problem right, her whole face lights up.

My A feels amazing, but watching Emma's confidence bloom? That hits different. Way different.

Later, I'm scrolling through this podcast talking about chasing happiness that Jake recommended. The guest says something that makes me pause: "Real joy doesn't come from personal achievements. It comes from lifting others up and finding meaning in small victories."

That's when it clicks. It's not just about my grades or nailing guitar solos or even getting that coffee shop gig. The best feeling I've had all week is watching Emma and Matt's smiles when things finally make sense for them.

Maybe happiness isn't something you chase for yourself. Maybe it's something you create for other people.

But now I'm lying here thinking—what if I could make this a regular thing? Not just random moments of helping Emma or Matt with homework, but actually making a difference in people's lives every day?

SIQ Tip: Bring others with me - be a happiness creator.

SUCCESS ANXIETY

Opening my gratitude journal tonight feels different. Today is rough—I forget my history homework, got into it with Tyler over something stupid, and Mom is stressed about work again.

But this is my thing. Three things I'm grateful for, no matter what. Today's list:

- The way the rain sounds during lunch – love it! ·
- Emma cracking up at her own terrible joke at dinner ·
- Finally nailing that tricky bridge in "Electric Nights"

Usually, writing these down flips a switch in my brain. Like hitting reset on a bad day. The problems don't disappear, but they shrink.

Tonight though? The reset button feels broken.

Midnight Static gets the gig at Brew & Bean. Our first real show! Jake's been texting the group chat nonstop about setlists and stage presence. Everyone's hyped, and I should be too. But all I can think about is: what if we suck? What if nobody shows up? What if I mess up in front of everyone and it's all over social media by morning?

The café used to feel like this cool dream. Now it feels like this massive thing hanging over my head, getting heavier every day. I keep refreshing their Instagram to see how many people usually come to shows. I'm analyzing every song we play, wondering if we're good enough.

When did chasing happiness become so stressful? I used to find joy in small stuff—nailing a new chord, helping Emma with homework, just vibing with my friends. Simple wins that feel real.

Now everything feels tied to this one night. Like if we bomb, all the progress I've made doesn't matter. The pressure is eating away at things I've been building.

I'm staring at tomorrow's blank page, and I'm scared to write in it. What if the three things don't work anymore? What if the bigger my dreams get, the smaller my daily joy becomes?

How do you stay happy when the stakes keep rising, and failure feels like it could crush everything you've worked for in one bad moment?

SIQ Tip: Gratitude isn't just a feeling; it's a powerful mental shift. If gratitude were a pill, it would be the most sought-after prescription for happiness and success.

CARING COSTS

My guitar feels heavier tonight. Not the actual weight—the weight of everything riding on next week's gig.

If we don't fill the place... if I mess up that solo... if my voice cracks on the high note...

The thoughts spiral like vultures. What started as pure excitement has twisted into this suffocating knot in my chest. Happiness feels like it's always one performance away, dangling just out of reach.

Uncle Rob came by today. He has this calm energy I wish I could bottle up. "You look ready to explode, kid," he says, settling onto my desk chair.

CHASING HAPPINESS

I can't hold it anymore. "What if nobody comes? What if I choke? This gig—it's literally everything to me."

Uncle Rob's smile is knowing, patient. "Pressure means you care and that's a beautiful thing. But don't let it own you." He leans forward. "Focus on what's in your control—your attitude, your preparation, your focus. The rest is just noise."

It's like he gives me permission to stop carrying the weight of outcomes I can't do anything about.

So this next week, I'm changing a couple things. Instead of obsessing over attendance numbers, I'm going to master my parts until my fingers move instinctively. Instead of reading reviews of other local bands, I'm focusing on *our* sound. I'm turning up the volume on my preparation.

Tonight is the night. Brew & Bean is packed—standing room only. Every riff lands exactly where it should. When we finish "Electric Nights," the applause feels like thunder. I float home, high on knowing I'd given everything I had.

But this morning? Art class happens.

Sitting there with my pathetic attempt at perspective drawing, I realize something disturbing. I'm completely fine with sucking at art. I don't even try. The thought that haunts me now: Why do I demand perfection from myself in music but accept mediocrity in other places? What makes some dreams worth the pressure while others get our leftover effort? Am I actually choosing what matters to me, or is the pressure choosing for me?

SIQ Tip: Use pressure to push myself forward instead of hold myself back.

SOCIAL BRUTALITY

I drag myself into art class today with my usual energy level: zero. I'm trash at drawing, always have been, and honestly? I've made peace with that.

But my friend Josh hits me with something his older brother told him: "If you have a positive mindset in whatever you're doing, your outcomes rise dramatically."

I almost laugh. Like, what's a good attitude gonna do for my stick figures? But I'd be lying if I didn't say curiosity gets me. What if he's right? So tomorrow, I'm gonna try something. I'm gonna walk into art class with one simple goal: find something—anything—worth learning. Just one thing.

Fast forward to the plot twist: I actually pick up two techniques. How to blend colors without making mud, and this shading trick that makes things look 3D. I add both to my gratitude journal that night. Maybe Josh isn't completely wrong.

Today I go all in. Instead of slouching in the back row, I sit closer to Ms. Newton. Ask questions. Actually look at what she's demonstrating instead of doodling band logos in my sketchbook.

And something weird happens—I get into it. Like, actually engaged. I find myself staying after class to finish this landscape piece. Blues and oranges mixing in ways that don't look like a kindergartner's fever dream.

For the first time ever, I'm proud of something I make in art class.

CHASING HAPPINESS

I feel so good about it that I post it on my story and Instagram. I spend hours on this thing between school and band practice. The colors actually look real; the perspective isn't completely broken.

At first, my friends come through with the usual support. "Yo looks good man!" "Since when do you do art?"

Then the comments get darker. Random people I barely know start roasting me. "Is this supposed to be good?" "This is a joke, right?" "Maybe stick to guitar lol."

Each comment feels like a punch. My stomach twists into knots. All that confidence I've built over two days? Gone. Shattered. Why does putting yourself out there always end with someone trying to tear you down?

SIQ Tip: Having a positive mindset is my single biggest competitive advantage today. It doesn't mean nothing will go wrong; it just means I'll be able to deal with things better when they do.

SISTER'S WISDOM
I'm sitting on my bed, phone in my hands, tears I can't stop. My art post—the landscape I was actually proud of—gets destroyed by random people online. "This looks so bad." "Is this a joke?" Each comment feels terrible.

Emma knocks and peeks in. "Mason, what's wrong?"

I don't want to admit I'm crying over Instagram comments, but she keeps asking. Finally I spill everything—how excited I was about the piece, how the comments crush me, and how stupid I feel for caring.

CHASING HAPPINESS

Emma listens with this serious expression I've never seen on her before. Then she asks the simplest question: "Why do you care what they think?"

"I don't know them, but—"

"Exactly. You don't like everyone either, right? And that's okay." She sits next to me, handing me another tissue. "You can't let people who don't know you ruin what makes you happy. If you like your art, focus on that. Not some random person's comment from someone you'll never meet."

She pauses, then adds quietly, "People who hurt others are usually hurting themselves."

When did my little sister get so smart?

Her words start sinking in. These strangers don't see the hours I spent mixing those colors. They don't know how art went from something I hated to something that actually matters to me. They're just voices behind screens.

In that moment, I decide I'm not letting random comments stop me from doing something that makes me proud.

Then today at school, everything changes again.

End of eighth grade's coming, and word's getting around that I'm not playing football in high school. My old teammates corner me by the lockers after last period.

"Heard you're not playing next year," Adam says, arms crossed.

"All into art and music now, huh?"

CHASING HAPPINESS

The way he says "art" makes it sound like a disease.

"Thought you were better than that, Mase," Connor adds.

"Guess you're just a fake after all."

Why does choosing what makes you happy always mean disappointing the people who knew you before?

SIQ Tip: Don't let 10 bad seconds of my day, ruin the remaining 86,390 I have left.

GROWING PAINS

I'm standing at my locker today, watching my old football crew walk by. The whispers aren't even subtle anymore. "Quitter." "Thought you were one of us."

Each word hits like a missed tackle. These guys—I've known them since elementary school. We've celebrated wins, cried over losses, spent countless afternoons running drills until we couldn't feel our legs.

But I make my choice. No football in high school. Instead, I'm going all in on music and art. Things that actually light something up inside me.

Football's fun, sure. But it never gives me the rush I get when I nail a difficult guitar solo or when a drawing actually looks like what I'm trying to create. When I'm playing music or sketching, I lose track of time. Football always feels like watching the clock.

Still, hearing "quitter" makes my stomach drop. Did I make the wrong call?

CHASING HAPPINESS

I called Josh tonight. He dropped baseball last year to focus on robotics, so I figure he'll get it.

"Dude, it's totally normal to change," he says, like it's obvious. "Everyone evolves. You've gotta chase what makes you happy, not what people expect. Otherwise, you're stuck doing something you hate, and that's just gonna make you miserable."

His words make a lot of sense. I've been so worried about disappointing my old teammates that I forgot the most important question: what do I actually want?

The truth? Football is something I was good at, but music and art are things I love. There's a difference, and I'm finally mature enough to see it.

I'm not a quitter. I'm just growing and am interested in some new things.

Fast forward to now—freshman year's been incredible. Midnight Static is killing it, my grades are solid, and I've found this balance between school and music that actually works. I feel more like myself than I ever did in shoulder pads.

But tonight I'm wondering—when you finally figure out who you are, why does it feel like you're constantly defending that choice to people who knew who you used to be?

SIQ Tip: Be okay pursuing what makes me happy and fills my buckets, not someone else's.

CHASING HAPPINESS

LOSING STABILITY

Everything is finally clicking. Freshman year's been incredible—grades are solid, Midnight Static just booked our second gig, and I've found this perfect balance between school and music. For the first time in forever, I feel like I have my life figured out.

Then Josh drops a bomb on me after band practice today.

"Mason, I need to tell you something," he says, looking really uncomfortable. "My dad got new orders. We're moving out of state."

I literally freeze. Josh isn't just my best friend—he's been my constant through everything. Football drama, every awkward middle school moment, figuring out who I am... He's the one who told me it was okay to not play football anymore when my old teammates called me a quitter.

"Wait, what? You're moving? When?"

"Next month."

I feel sick. The thought of not having Josh around—no more hanging out after school, no more late-night text conversations about everything and nothing and chatting about it the next day, no more having someone who just gets it—I can't even process it.

Josh has been my rock through every major change in my life. When I was spiraling about the café gig, he helped me see clearly.

"Dude, I don't know what I'm gonna do without you," I tell him, and I mean it. For the first time in months, I feel completely lost.

Josh gives me this weak smile. "You'll figure it out. You always do."

But walking home today, the weight of it all hits me. Just when I think I have things figured out, life throws this curveball. It's like the universe is testing me—can you stay happy when the people who matter most disappear from your life?

I've spent so much time learning to find joy in the small moments, to build confidence, to choose what makes me happy. But what happens when happiness depends on people, and those people leave?

NOT ENOUGH

I'm staring at Josh's last text: *"I'll miss you, man. Promise we'll stay in touch."*

The house feels impossibly quiet. Like the whole world shifts and forgets to tell me. My best friend—my only real friend— is gone. Just like that.

The weeks leading up to his move are torture. We hang out, try to act normal, but there's this countdown ticking in my head the whole time. Every laugh feels borrowed. Every inside joke feels like it might be our last.

Now he's actually gone. No more biking to school together. No more late-night gaming sessions where we'd talk about everything—band stuff, stupid crushes, what we want to do with our lives. The spot where we used to sit and play video games is just empty space now.

I keep telling myself we'll stay friends, that distance doesn't matter. But it already feels different. His texts are shorter. There's this time delay that makes conversations feel forced. The ache in my chest won't go away. And tonight makes everything worse.

Dinner is the Emma show again. Mom and Dad can't stop gushing about her latest academic achievement—some advanced math thing she's doing in fifth grade. "We're so proud of you, sweetheart!" "You're so smart!" "You're going to do amazing things!"

I sit there pushing my food around, completely invisible. Mom barely even asks how my day was. When I mention that Midnight Static might get another gig, Dad just nods and turns back to praising Emma's homework.

My throat gets tight. Eyes start stinging. It doesn't matter how hard I work or what I accomplish—it's never enough for them. Never worthy of the attention Emma gets just for existing. First Josh leaves. Now I'm realizing I've been invisible at home this whole time.

I slip away from the table before anyone notices I'm gone. Which, let's be honest, they probably don't.

WRONG PLACES
Same dinner scene as always. Mom and Dad practically glow while they praise Emma's perfect report card.

CHASING HAPPINESS

"We're so proud of you, sweetheart!" The usual parade of compliments while I push food around my plate, trying to ignore that familiar weight crushing my chest.

No matter what I do—music, art, decent grades—I'm always in her shadow. Always the afterthought. But tonight, surprisingly ends up being different.

Mom knocks on my door after I get done with my homework and sits on my bed. "Mason, I've noticed you've been down lately," she says softly. "I want you to know that we do see you, and we are incredibly proud of you too. You're talented and creative in ways that amaze us."

I almost don't believe her. But then she hands me an envelope. Inside are two tickets to see OneRepublic next month. ONE REPUBLIC! My favorite band ever!

"Seriously?!" My voice cracks like I'm twelve again.

Mom smiles. "Just you and me kiddo. I thought you deserved something special for all your hard work."

For the first time in so long, I feel this spark of happiness at home. Maybe I'm not completely invisible after all. Maybe they have been paying attention to the things that matter to me.

But here's the weird part—just as that weight starts lifting off my shoulders, a new pressure creeps in.

It's Victor. The lead singer of this other local band that sometimes jams with us. He's older, cooler, the guy everyone listens to when he talks. And for some reason, I find myself desperately wanting his approval.

114

CHASING HAPPINESS

Every time I mess up a note or he gives even the slightest critique, it hits harder than it should. Like his opinion somehow matters more than Jake's or anyone else's in the group. When he nodded at my solo last week, I felt this rush that's almost as good as getting those concert tickets.

Why do I care so much what Victor thinks? Why is his validation suddenly everything to me?

MIRROR MOMENT
I've been chasing Victor's approval for months now. Ever since he started jamming with us occasionally, I want his validation more than anyone else's. He has this effortless confidence that makes everyone gravitate toward him, and I find myself second-guessing every riff, every vocal run, waiting for some sign that he thinks I'm good enough.

That sign never comes.

But something weird has happened over the past few weeks. As freshman year winds down, I start realizing something: Victor's approval isn't coming, and maybe it doesn't need to.

Every practice, every late-night session, every time I push through a difficult song—I prove something way more important. To myself. I stick with this band, put in the work, improve dramatically since Josh left. That validation I was hunting for? I think it's inside me the whole time.

I'm proud of how far I've come, especially after losing my best friend and feeling invisible at home. This music isn't for Victor or anyone else to validate—it's mine.

Today, after rehearsal, I notice something else.

CHASING HAPPINESS

I catch a glimpse of myself in the bathroom mirror at the community center. My shirt clings awkwardly to my stomach, and for the first time ever, I really don't like what I see. My stomach isn't flat like Victor's. My arms aren't toned. I feel... fat.

I've always eaten whatever I wanted—pizza after practice, late-night snacks while doing homework. Never cared about my appearance before. But today it hits different I guess. It bothers me in a way I can't shake.

Why am I suddenly so focused on my body? Where does this come from?

Standing there staring at my reflection, this new worry starts gnawing at me—one I have no idea how to handle. Is this what growing up feels like? Trading one insecurity for another?

Just when I figure out that validation comes from within, my brain finds a new way to make me feel not good enough.

DAD'S STORIES

The mirror becomes my enemy. Every time I catch my reflection, all I see is what's wrong—stomach too soft, arms too thin. The word "fat" keeps echoing in my head like a broken record.

I start skipping lunch at school, thinking that will help. All it does is make me hangry and miserable. I've been snapping at Jake and the guys over stupid stuff, pushing everyone away. Even music feels suffocating now.

CHASING HAPPINESS

Tonight, I stormed out of band practice after losing it over a missed chord change that doesn't even matter. I come home and slam my door so hard the walls shake.

Dad knocks a few minutes later. "What's going on with you?"

I almost brush him off with the usual "nothing," but something makes me crack. Maybe it's how tired I am of carrying this alone. I spill everything—the mirror obsession, the body shame, feeling like I need to look completely different to matter.

Dad leans against my doorframe, quiet for a moment. Then he says, "I get it. I've been there."

He tells me stories I've never heard before. About being skinny in high school, getting picked on, spending hours doing push-ups in his room trying to get bigger. About the summer he barely ate because he thought he was too heavy. About learning that beating yourself up never actually changes anything.

"It's not about hating what you see," he says. "It's about working with it."

I don't expect his words to relate so much, but they do. Dad gets it in a way I never knew.

As freshman year ends, I stop skipping meals and start focusing on healthier ways to feel better about myself. Not starving myself, but actually taking care of my body.

Something surprising happens in the process—I start attracting new people into my life. Including this girl Kaily who seems to show up everywhere I go lately.

CHASING HAPPINESS

SIQ Tip: Chasing happiness means learning that the way I treat myself sets the tone for how others treat me.

LAKE TEMPTATION
I can't believe my luck. Everywhere I turn, Kaily's there—at school, the park, even Jake's birthday party last weekend. I'm not questioning how it keeps happening; I'm just happy it is.

We click instantly. Music, life, dreams—we talk about everything. By the end of that first real conversation, I feel a spark I'd hoped for but never thought I'd actually experience.

As summer approaches, we grow closer. Constant texting, hanging out at our favorite spots around town, making plans for break. For the first time in forever, I feel like I've found something real. Someone real.

But as things heat up between us, so does the social scene.

Tonight at the lake party, surrounded by pounding music and flashing phone lights, everything changes. A group of older kids I barely know corner us near the bonfire pit.

"You two look way too innocent," one of them laughs, phone already out and recording. "We're doing this viral challenge—you have to take these edibles or chug this entire bottle."

My heart starts racing. I've never been in a situation like this. The music feels too loud, the lights too bright. My palms get sweaty. For the first time in months, I have no idea what to say.

CHASING HAPPINESS

I glance at Kaily, who looks mortified. Her eyes are wide, panicked. The group is still standing there, phone cameras pointed at us, and other kids are starting to gather around.

The pressure is building fast. Everyone is definitely watching now, some pulling out their own phones. I feel like I'm back in middle school, facing down my football teammates when I quit. But this is different. This feels like our choices, our boundaries, are about to become everyone's entertainment.

Kaily grabs my hand, squeezing it tight. Whatever we decide, we'll decide together.

But what do you do when saying no might make you look boring, but saying yes means letting strangers pressure you into something you're not ready for—all for their social media content?

FUTURE FEAR

Kaily and I are inseparable all summer. Swimming at the lake, trading inside jokes, sharing dreams under the stars. Everything feels perfect—until tonight.

What's supposed to be a fun sleepover at Emma's house turns into something else entirely. Just our close friend group, watching movies and eating way too much pizza. But then Emma's older brother comes home with some of his friends.

We're all sitting in the living room when they walk in, already being loud and obnoxious. One of them looks at Kaily and me cuddled up on the couch and smirks.

"You two are so cute it's gross," he says, pulling out his phone. "Let's spice things up—make out for thirty seconds and we'll leave you alone. Or we can make this sleepover way more interesting."

My heart sinks. This is supposed to be our safe space—just us and our friends having innocent fun. I suddenly feel like I'm back at that first party not long ago, when someone tried pressuring us into something we weren't ready for. We didn't do anything then, but this feels worse because we're trapped here.

I glance at Kaily—she looks mortified, the same wide-eyed panic I remember from just a couple months ago. But we've grown since then. We've learned to trust each other.

My mind races. This isn't some random party we can leave. This is Emma's house, our friend group watching. One wrong move and our private relationship becomes entertainment for people who shouldn't even be here.

"Nah," I say finally, standing up and taking Kaily's hand. "We're good. Maybe you guys should find something else to do."

Kaily exhales, relief flooding her face. Emma steps in too, telling her brother to back off.

The rest of the night is awkward, but we get through it together. The weight of that moment stays with both of us.

Fast forward to now—fall semester of senior year. Kaily and I are still together, still strong. But there's this big question looming over us that we can't ignore: What happens after high school?

Will our paths stay aligned, or are we destined to split apart? College applications are due soon. She's talking about schools on the East Coast. I'm looking at programs closer to home for music production.

The scariest part isn't the distance—it's wondering if we'll still be the same people who chose each other at those parties, or if we'll grow into different versions of ourselves.

DIFFERENT DREAMS
Kaily and I have been through everything together—late-night talks, awkward first dates, road trips, high school milestones. We've shared dreams about college and believe, with the certainty only our love can bring, that we'll face the future side by side.

But as spring approaches, reality hits. The acceptance letters arrive, and with them, the kind of uncertainty neither of us is ready for.

I open my letter first: University of Washington—my number one choice. I should be over the moon, but the look in Kaily's eyes stops me cold.

"I didn't get in," she whispers, handing me her letter. "But I got into Utah... and that small liberal arts school in Idaho."

My chest tightens. Utah. Idaho. They aren't part of the plan. Not *our* plan. I reach for her hand, but she's already wiping away tears. This is supposed to be exciting—celebrating our futures—but now it feels like the end of something so much bigger.

Over the next few weeks, we try to talk through it. Kaily says she'll consider Utah, maybe we can do long-distance, but every conversation ends the same way—with us staring at each other, realizing that our paths aren't aligned anymore.

Tonight, by the lake where our relationship began, we hold each other in silence, the weight of our first heartbreak sinking in.

"We'll always have this, right?" Kaily asks, her voice shaking.

"Yeah," I say, barely holding it together. "But we have to let go."

We cry, and kiss one last time, knowing it's goodbye.

As I drive home alone for the first time in years, my heart feels hollow. The car is too quiet. My phone has no new messages. The future I'd imagined—us studying together, visiting each other's campuses, growing up together—evaporates.

I keep telling myself this is what growing up looks like. That sometimes loving someone means letting them chase their dreams, even when those dreams don't include you.

But right now, sitting in my empty room, it just feels like I lost the best thing I ever had.

REBUILDING MYSELF
This summer is about finding my footing. After breaking up with Kaily—my first serious relationship—the world feels emptier. We'd shared everything: hopes, dreams, late-night talks about the future. Now I have to face all of that alone.

CHASING HAPPINESS

At first, I'm not sure how to handle it. The silence is overwhelming. But slowly, as weeks pass, I find some solace in it. Being single gives me time to focus on myself—something I haven't done in years. I pour energy into music, pick up sketching again, find small moments of peace in simply being alone. The ache is still there, but it isn't crushing anymore.

By the time I move to Seattle for college, I feel more grounded, but the transition is still daunting. New city, new state, no familiar faces. Everything feels foreign and intimidating.

But orientation week changes that for me. I meet a group of people in my dorm who share some of my interests—music, art, and a sense of adventure. There's Abraham, who plays bass and knows every coffee shop in the city. Sarah, an art major who sketches constantly and has this infectious laugh. And there's Kevin, who's into music production and already has connections at local venues.

They become my lifeline, pulling me into spontaneous trips around the city, late-night jam sessions in the common room, and long talks about life that remind me of the conversations I used to have with Kaily—but different. New perspectives, new dreams.

For the first time since the breakup, I can breathe again. I'm rebuilding myself piece by piece, discovering parts of me that got lost in being with someone.

The weird thing is, I'm starting to enjoy who I am when I'm just me. Not Mason-and-Kaily, not Mason-trying-to-impress-someone. Just Mason.

CHASING HAPPINESS

SIQ Tip: People who introduce me to new ways of thinking and new ways of seeing life are so important.

DROWNING AGAIN

I start my freshman year of college feeling nervous but excited—a fresh start in a new city. Yeah I miss home and the familiar faces from high school, but getting to know some new people helps me a ton.

When I doubt my guitar skills, Abraham pushes me to jam with him and shows me techniques I'd never tried. When I'm completely lost in my engineering homework, Sarah doesn't just give me answers—she sits with me for three hours breaking down the concepts until they actually click. "You're not stupid," she keeps saying. "This stuff is just hard at first."

When I question whether I belong in my music production classes, Kevin reminds me why I chose this path in the first place. And when I'm spiraling about everything, he drags me out: "Dude, you need to touch grass. Let's go get boba and pretend we're not dying inside."

Between impromptu jam sessions, weekend hikes, and late-night study sessions, I feel like I'm finally finding my rhythm again. My first taste of real independence is freeing. For the first time since breaking up with Kaily, I feel whole—like I'm moving forward with my own life, surrounded by people who genuinely want to see me succeed.

Having a tribe that builds you up instead of tearing you down is everything. They celebrate my wins, help me through losses, and push me to be better without making me feel inadequate.

But as the semester wears on, things begin piling up. Classes are harder than expected, and juggling school with my part-time job at the campus coffee shop drains me. The excitement of college life slowly gives way to creeping pressure. Papers, projects, and late shifts blur together.

Even my supportive friend group starts feeling like another obligation I can't manage.

Late last night, staring at a mountain of unfinished assignments, it hits me: *I'm drowning.* And I have no idea how I'm going to survive the rest of the semester at this pace.

MIND AGAINST ME

I'm sitting in my dorm, buried in assignments with deadlines looming and exhaustion weighing me down. College, once exciting, has become suffocating—school, work, and friends all pulling me in different directions. I can't find a reason to be happy because I'm constantly stressed about disappointing someone or falling behind somewhere.

Desperate for some kind of clarity, I call Dad.

"I'm drowning," I admit. "I don't know how to handle all of this."

Dad pauses, then asks, "What's overwhelming you the most right now?"

I frown. "Everything. I don't even know where to start."

"Okay," he says calmly. "What's one thing you can control right now that would make the biggest impact?"

CHASING HAPPINESS

That question makes me pause. I think for a second. "Maybe I can cut back on work," I murmur, surprising even myself.

"And what would that free up for you?"

"Time... and energy, I guess."

After hanging up, I realize Dad's right—focusing on just one thing that could make the biggest impact could help me find a little more balance instead of chasing something in every direction at once. I cut back my coffee shop hours, which allows me to prioritize my studies, and I actually start to feel a weight lift. My grades improve, I have more time with friends, and I don't constantly feel exhausted.

For a few weeks, I think I've figured out the secret to college and my life: just manage your priorities better.

But then, out of nowhere, something new creeps in. Last night my friends invite me to this party downtown, and I freeze. My chest tightens and my heart starts racing. The idea of going out feels terrifying. I can't explain it—anxiety has never been an issue before, and certainly not when I'm out with my friends.

I suddenly don't want to see anyone. I just want to hide in my room and avoid all human contact.

Why is this happening now? Just when I think I have a good balance, my brain decides socializing is the enemy.

GETTING HELP WORKS
I've always been the laid-back, go-with-the-flow kind of guy. I love hanging out with friends, playing music, exploring

CHASING HAPPINESS

Seattle. But out of nowhere, I start feeling anxious—like, really anxious.

That night when my friends text me to come out, I froze. My chest tightened, my heart raced, and suddenly the thought of being around people terrified me. I make excuses, bail, and sit alone in my dorm wondering: *Where did this come from? Why me? Why now?*

Weeks go by, and the anxiety gets worse. I withdraw a lot, avoiding my friends, feeling more isolated every day. I think it will go away, but the pressure keeps crushing me. My norm feels completely hijacked by this invisible force I can't control.

Finally, after another week of feeling trapped by my own thoughts, I do something I never imagined—I book an appointment with a therapist through the campus health center.

At first, it's uncomfortable and embarrassing. Talking to a stranger about my fears feels weird. But slowly, working through my anxiety starts to help. Dr. Watson is able to help me unpack what's happening, and asks some questions that make me think differently about myself.

It doesn't just go away overnight, but it's a start. I begin understanding that anxiety isn't something that's wrong with me—and it's something I can learn to manage. Most importantly, I realize I'm not the only one who deals with this.

Some breathing techniques and cognitive exercises help. But mostly, just having someone validate that what I'm experiencing is real and treatable—that helps the most.

CHASING HAPPINESS

Just as I'm getting back on track, I meet Emily. She's in my music theory class, and we get paired for a project. She's different—easy to talk to, kind, genuinely interested in my thoughts about music and life.

For the first time in months, I feel excited about someone. Not anxious, not overwhelmed—just genuinely happy to spend time with another person again. Things seem like they're falling into place, and I'm learning that getting help isn't giving up on happiness—it's fighting for it.

SIQ Tip: To get places I've never been, sometimes I need to do things I've never done.

PROTECTING MY PROGRESS

Things feel like they're finally coming together. After months of battling anxiety, meeting Emily has been like a breath of fresh air. We connect so easily—long talks, late-night drives, everything feels perfect. But then, some cracks start to show.

This morning, Emily texts me to skip class and hang out. When I meet her, she pulls a bottle of vodka out of her bag, smiling like it's a joke.

"Let's have a drink," she says, offering me the bottle.

I freeze and just stare at her. "It's 9 a.m.," I say, my voice barely above a whisper.

But Emily shrugs, taking a swig. "What does it matter? Just loosen up, Mase."

It isn't the first time. I've started noticing how often she drinks—before class, after class, on weekends. It isn't just fun; it's an escape, and it scares me. As much as I care for her, the truth is sinking in: Emily is spiraling, and I can't save her.

My friends Abraham and Sarah have been trying to tell me for weeks. "She's dragging you down," Sarah says gently. "You've been so much happier when she's not around." Abraham nods. "You deserve someone who builds you up, not someone who pulls you into their mess."

I didn't want to hear it then, but they're right. Emily isn't building me up—she's slowly tearing down the progress I've made with therapy, with my anxiety, with finding my balance.

Last night, after another heart-wrenching conversation where she gets defensive about her drinking, I make the hardest decision: I walk away. She isn't ready to change, and I decide I can't be pulled down with her.

As I leave her dorm, the guilt weighs on me. But I know I have to protect myself. Being brave enough to separate from someone who brings you down, even when you care about them, might be one of the hardest things to do.

I feel a little relief though, a sense of calm. Then my Mom calls about holiday plans. Her voice cracks.

"Mason, there's something I need to tell you," she says slowly. "Your dad and I... we're getting a divorce."

First Emily, now this?!

ACCEPTING WHAT IS

I'm dreading calling Mom about holiday plans. I haven't been home in a while, and I finally dial, expecting the usual questions about school and life. But her voice is different—strained.

"Mason, your dad and I... we're getting a divorce," she says, the words hanging heavy over the line.

I sit in silence, the weight sinking in. I've always thought of my parents as solid, the kind of couple that never wavers.

Now everything I know feels shaken. Over the next few weeks, I struggle with the news, trying to make sense of it—why now? Why them?

But as winter break rolls around, something unexpected happens. Despite the split, Mom and Dad are calm. They aren't fighting, and in their own ways, they seem happier. More relaxed. More like themselves than I've seen them in years.

Watching them navigate their situation with such grace makes me realize something: not all endings are bad. Sometimes what looks like failure is actually a step toward something better. They aren't giving up on happiness—they're choosing it, just in a different way than I expected.

I learn to accept it, understanding that their decision isn't about failure but about finding their own sense of peace. They'd tried to make it work for years, but sometimes love means letting go of what isn't serving you anymore.

Their decision to choose separating amicably over pretending helps me find my own comfort level with the situation. I guess families don't have to look perfect to be loving. Sometimes the most loving thing is admitting when something isn't working.

Just as I'm starting to feel genuinely at peace with everything, I bump into Tyler at a holiday gathering. After catching up, he asks the dreaded question: "So, what are you gonna do after college?"

I freeze, the weight of uncertainty crashing back in. *What am I going to do?* I have no answer. And suddenly, that familiar feeling of being lost returns, threatening the inner peace I'd just found.

SIQ Tip: Embrace the unknown. Focus on making the best of my choices, not focusing so much on making the single best choice.

NO CLEAR PATH

I'm standing awkwardly at the holiday party, catching up with old friends when the question hits me out of nowhere: "So, what are you gonna do after college?"

I freeze. The truth is, I have no idea. My heart races as I respond with something vague about "Ah you know, I'm figuring it out," but the question gnaws at me for a while after the conversation ends. What am I going to do? Everyone else seems to have a plan—grad school, job offers, clear paths forward. But me? I feel completely lost.

The unknown has always terrified me. When I was pursuing things through music, art, relationships, at least I knew what direction I was heading. Now I'm staring into this void after graduation, and it feels like everything I've worked toward leads to... nothing concrete.

Later at home, I bring it up with my parents. To my surprise, they don't seem worried at all.

"You don't need to have it all figured out right now," Dad says. "You're doing well in school, and that's what matters. Enjoy this time—you won't always have the freedom to explore."

Mom chimes in. "You have time, Mason. Focus on what you enjoy. The rest will come as you work your way through your experiences."

Their words are a relief, like a weight lifting off my chest. I don't need to have all the answers yet. Maybe fearing the unknown is normal, and maybe that's okay. The pressure eases, and for the first time in weeks, I feel like I can breathe.

Their perspective helps me realize that wanting to do big things in life doesn't always require knowing exactly where you're going—sometimes it just requires trusting that you'll figure it out along the way.

And just when things start to settle, I face a new blow. After weeks of waiting, I receive an email: *We regret to inform you that you have not been selected for the summer internship.*

My heart sinks. It's the first opportunity I'd truly cared about—a music production company I'd dreamed of working for. Now that door shuts, and the unknown feels scarier than ever.

CHASING HAPPINESS

SHIFT, DON'T QUIT

I stare blankly at the email. "We regret to inform you..." The words hit harder than I expect. The internship at the music production company feels like the *perfect* opportunity—my first real step toward a future I'm excited about. Now it feels like the rug has been pulled out from under me.

Frustration swirls in my head. I've worked so hard, convinced this is the door that will open for me. But then something Dr. Watson once said flickers in my mind: "Rejection isn't the end. It's information. It shows you where to shift."

I take a deep breath. This isn't the end of my journey. It doesn't erase everything I've accomplished—my grades, my growth, my music skills. Slowly, the sting of rejection dulls. Maybe this is just information telling me to look elsewhere, try harder, or explore different paths I haven't considered.

I know I have to shift my focus, keep moving. I'll figure it out. I always do.

But as days pass, new doubts creep in—deeper and harder to shake. Outwardly, I keep up my usual front: confident, relaxed, the guy who has a plan. But inside, I'm unraveling.

Will I ever find someone I care about as much as I had with Kaily? Am I destined to feel like I'm constantly chasing something, always just out of reach? Every time I get close to something good—a relationship, an opportunity, inner peace—something seems to knock me back to square one.

I can't talk to anyone about it, not even Abraham or Sarah. How do you explain that you're tired of trying so hard just to feel okay? That happiness feels like this elusive thing you're always almost catching but never quite holding onto?

Maybe the real information from this rejection isn't about career paths—maybe it's about learning that happiness isn't something you achieve once and keep forever.

HIDING PRIVATE STRUGGLES

I've become a master at wearing masks. On the outside, I'm the fun, easygoing guy who always has a smile ready for friends and family. But inside, I wrestle with deeper, gnawing questions that never seem to quiet down.

I still don't feel like I've moved on from Kaily. Can't shake the thought that I might never feel that kind of connection again. Even worse, happiness feels like this distant, unreachable thing—something other people seem to have naturally, but not me.

The challenge of maintaining this public face while drowning privately is exhausting. When Abraham asks how I'm doing, I automatically say "good" even when I'm not. When Sarah notices I seem off, I crack a joke to deflect. It's easier than explaining that I feel like I'm failing at the one thing everyone else makes look effortless—just being happy.

As junior year rolls around, the questions grow louder. *What if I'm just never going to feel satisfied? How many more years will it take to get there?*

One restless night, I come across a podcast. The host talks about happiness in a way I've never considered before. "Happiness," he explains, "isn't some grand destination to chase—it's about moments along the way. Not an endpoint, but something you can experience in the process of living."

CHASING HAPPINESS

The idea sticks with me. I start trying to reframe things, focus on small, good moments instead of constantly searching for the next big win. It helps, a little. But the restlessness doesn't disappear completely.

Then, at a party last night, something unexpected happens. A friend offers me something—a pill, something to "loosen up" and stop overthinking.

For a second, I hesitate. I know it's a bad idea, but I'm so tired of the questions, tired of the weight inside me, tired of pretending everything is fine when it isn't.

Maybe this could help. Maybe it could quiet the noise in my head, make me feel as carefree as everyone thinks I already am.

I take the pill.

HUMAN & FLAWED
I'm sitting on the edge of my bed, staring at the floor. The party is a blur, but one moment stands out with brutal clarity—I took the pill. I've always told myself I wouldn't, that drugs aren't for me. But in that split second, I was so tired of fighting the emptiness inside, and I gave in.

Now the guilt crashes over me in waves. I can't believe I did it. I feel disgusted with myself, like I let everything slip. It isn't just taking the drug—it's thinking it might actually fix something.

Yesterday I booked an appointment with Dr. Watson, filled with shame and embarrassment. "I feel like I've ruined everything," I confess, my voice barely a whisper.

CHASING HAPPINESS

She listens calmly, then asks, "Do you think one mistake defines who you are?"

I shake my head, but deep down, part of me believes it does. She helps me work through the guilt, reminding me that mistakes are part of life—not something to hide from, but something to learn from.

"You can't hate yourself for what's already done," she says. "The key is learning to love yourself, even when you stumble."

Those words stick with me. It isn't going to be easy, but maybe loving myself—mistakes and all—is the way forward. Maybe the private struggle I've been carrying isn't about finding perfect happiness, but about accepting that I'm human and flawed and still worthy of my own compassion.

I've spent so much energy hating parts of myself: the anxiety, the loneliness, the desperate need for connection, the moment I took that pill. But what if all those parts are just... me? What if loving myself means embracing the messy reality of who I am instead of chasing some perfect version?

But as I leave therapy, a thought looms in my mind: How do you learn to love yourself when you've spent years picking yourself apart?

SIQ Tip: Self-love isn't about pretending I'm perfect—it's about showing myself the same compassion I'd give a friend who made the same mistake. My future self deserves that.

SOCIAL MEDIA DETOX

I sat across from Dr. Watson today, talking about something that's been haunting me for months: how hard it is to accept myself—all of myself, mistakes included.

"I keep thinking if I could just fix everything, I'd be happier," I admit.

She smiles gently. "You don't need to be perfect to be happy, Mason. Loving yourself means embracing the messy parts, too. You've made mistakes, sure, but that doesn't define who you are. Start small—be kind to yourself, even in moments you feel you don't deserve it."

Over the next few weeks, I work on forgiving myself—taking deep breaths when feeling overwhelmed, reminding myself that one mistake doesn't undo my worth. I start noticing more little victories, moments where I feel lighter and accomplished.

But something else is nagging at me: social media. It's like a constant reminder of everything I'm not—every scroll brings feelings of inadequacy. Seeing everyone's highlight reels while I'm still figuring out basic self-acceptance feels toxic.

So I decide to cut back. I'll use my phone less and spend more time with people who actually make me feel good about myself.

With more time on my hands, I begin reconnecting with real life. I go out more, rediscover old hobbies, and even join a new music group on campus.

That's when Maddie comes into my life. But unlike the typical romantic spark, our connection throws me off balance.

Maddie is everything I'm not—fearless, bold, unapologetically herself. She pushes me out of my comfort zone, challenging me in ways that unsettle me.

Where I overthink everything, she acts on instinct. Where I play it safe, she takes risks. Being around her makes me question whether my careful approach to life is actually holding me back.

THE RIPPLE EFFECT

I met Maddie during a casual night out with friends, and she quickly flips my world upside down. She's adventurous, fearless, always pushing boundaries—everything I'm not. But something about her energy pulls me in, making me want to break out of my comfort zone.

A few weeks later, Maddie suggests kayaking. I've never been on the water before, at least not like this. The idea of navigating the river's twists and turns makes me uneasy, but Maddie's enthusiasm is hard to resist.

"Come on," she grins, handing me a paddle. "You'll love it."

She's right. As we paddle through the calm waters, I feel the tension I usually carry start to dissolve. The rhythm of the paddle, the sound of water lapping against the kayak—it's peaceful in a way I haven't expected. But the occasional rapids? Those give me an adrenaline rush I didn't know I craved.

With Maddie laughing beside me as we navigate through choppy sections, it becomes more than just an activity. It's freeing. For the first time in months, I'm not overthinking every move or worrying about what could go wrong. I'm just present, focused on the water and the moment.

Soon, kayaking becomes our thing—a hobby that gives me a sense of adventure I haven't experienced before. I love how it makes me feel: alive, confident, capable of something completely new.

Being with Maddie shows me parts of myself I'd forgotten existed. The part that can take risks, that can find joy in uncertainty, that doesn't need to have everything planned out to feel okay.

But as our friendship deepens, I start noticing something else. Maddie isn't just adventurous—she's restless. Always looking for the next thrill, the next boundary to push. Sometimes her fearlessness feels less like courage and more like she's running from something.

I find myself wondering: Is this the kind of adventure that leads to happiness, or the kind that keeps you from ever sitting still long enough to find it?

A LASTING THOUGHT
FROM: NATURE
TO: YOU

There's a simple experiment nature shows us about how we learn limits, specifically when they exist mentally.

If you put fleas in a glass jar and close the lid, they'll jump and hit it over and over.

After a while, something changes. They stop jumping so high. They learn where the ceiling is.

But here's the surprising truth that gets passed on: when the lid is eventually removed, the fleas still won't jump out.

They could. They just... don't.

And even their offspring—fleas who've never hit the lid—will only jump as high as they've seen others go.

It's not about ability. It's about belief.

That's what *Starting* is helping you understand through short stories.

Don't wait for breakdowns to start building yourself back up: learn to train your mental skills before life convinces you to shrink.

Mental skills aren't just something you should reach for when things fall apart. They're the things that can help keep you from falling apart in the first place.

Self-talk. Focus. Emotional regulation. Preparation.
Resilience.

They don't make life easy—but they do make you ready.

Because the lid?
Most of the time, it's not real.
It's a story you tell yourself. A habit you learned and never
questioned. A belief someone else passed down without even
realizing it.

So here's your challenge:
Don't wait for life to shake your jar.
Build now—before you think you need it.
So when life takes the lid off...
You're already jumping and prepared to get out!

*If you or someone you know is interested in investing in one
of the few things no one can ever take away from you, your
mental skills, subscribe to Mental on your preferred podcast
platform. It's a commitment, a movement, an investment; in
our future, for our future. And it's updated weekly!*